We're Not Robots

SUNY series, Early Childhood Education:
Inquiries and Insights

Mary A. Jensen, editor

We're Not Robots

The Voices of Daycare Providers

Enid Elliot

❖

Foreword by Janet Gonzalez-Mena

State University of New York Press

Published by
State University of New York Press, Albany

For information, address State University of New York Press,
194 Washington Avenue, Suite 305, Albany, NY 12210–2384

Production by Diane Ganeles
Marketing by Anne M. Valentine

Library of Congress Cataloging-in-Publication Data

Elliot, Enid, 1947–
    We're not robots: the voices of daycare providers / Enid Elliot, foreword by
Janet Gonzalez-Mena.
        p. cm. — (SUNY series, early childhood education)
    Includes bibliographical references and index.
    ISBN-13: 978–0–7914–6941–5 (hardcover : alk. paper)
    ISBN-10: 0–7914–6941–7 (hardcover : alk. paper)
    ISBN-13: 978–0–7914–6942–2 (pbk : alk. paper)
    ISBN-10: 0–7914–6942–5 (pbk : alk. paper)
    1. Child care workers—Psychology. 2. Infants—Care—Psychological aspects.
3. Toddlers—Care—Psychological aspects. I. Title. II. Series.

HQ778.5.E54 2007
362.71'2—dc22

2005037860

10 9 8 7 6 5 4 3 2 1

Contents

Acknowledgments

Though a solitary journey, the road to this book has not been travelled alone. I have had good companions for whom I am grateful. Margie Mayfield helped me get started; Alison Preece and Antoinette Oberg provided insights, warm support, and helped me come to an end. Jinny Hayes, Frances Ricks, Martha Haylor provided support along the way, as did Carol Anne Wien.

Friends kept me going with encouragement, help, and feedback. I particularly want to thank Heather Kay and Janet Gonzalez-Mena, who read innumerable bits and pieces of this book and never lost enthusiasm. I want to acknowledge the caregivers with whom I have worked and learned. I continue to learn from them, each one is an inspiration: Jackie Hurst, Jan Carrie, Deborah Maunder, Marta Pascolin, Wendy Ready, Serina Labh-Rizzo, Ruth Gale, Mariah Evans, Nancy Sturdiman, Shirley-Lee Doucette, Michelle Chequer, Donna-Lynn Thorpe. My doctoral group of fellow scholars, Sally Kimpson, Wendy Donawa, Pat Rasmussen, Heather Hermanson, and Joan Boyce, gave me courage. My thanks also go to Betty Jones, Joe Tobin, Alicia Lieberman, to the Sisters of Saint Anne (Beverly Mitchell and Jessica Bell), Muriel and Janna Ginsberg, Renie Grosser, Chrystal Kleiman, the Harveys, Jesse Dillard.

I thank my family, for they have been my spirit guides. My mother, Nancy Haskins Elliot, is always nearby, as is my brother, John Elliot. They know I am grateful. My father, David Elliot, encourages by his example, his editing, and his love. My sister and pal, Nan Elliot, has kept me going on many levels. My children, Jessica, David, Mari, and Isaac helped me keep my perspective.

My dear sister-friend, Kristin Watson, has given me many wise words. "The relationship has become a partnership" and without my partner, Rick Kool, who manifested endless love, patience, and technical know-how in this whole process I doubt I would have finished.

Foreword

" I don't know how you do it" is a remark often made by parents and others to infant-toddler caregivers. Enid Elliot sought to find the answer to that question, and this book is the result. In a word, the answer is "caring."

As Nel Noddings and Carol Gilligan brought caring into the fields of morals, education, and character development, so Enid Elliot is bringing the subject into early childhood education and care. I predict *We're Not Robots* will make an impact on the field of infant-toddler care and beyond. By making a strong case for caring relationships and showing how they work from the perspective of the caregivers, Elliot brings up the many complexities, tensions, and rewards, as well as some deep questions for North American society. The book not only questions, but provides answers as well, but by the end Elliot goes all the way to challenging us to think way beyond the universal child and child development.

One can't help but appreciate the wide variety of caregiving experience that Elliot brings to this book, having been a caregiver herself in Turkey, New York, Berkeley, California, as well as in Vancouver and Victoria in British Columbia. How many researchers have actually been in the shoes of their subjects? Enid has done what she's writing about and has felt the tensions she's studied. She is truly an expert, from all angles. Further, she used the skills she learned as a caregiver to study other caregivers, skills such as listening carefully, observing closely, and reflecting deeply. Throughout the book she shows how during her interviews she is able to move from judging to wondering—an important skill for infant-toddler caregivers as well as researchers.

Elliot brings to light the invisible and gives voice to the unvoiced through storytelling and powerful personal statements. Throughout the book we feel the emotional pulls of those who work with the youngest children. Instead of emotional distance, the usual solution to being tugged by feelings, Elliot shows case after case of caregivers in caring relationships with babies where emotions are fully present. She documents that creating caring relationships demands deep involvement leading to attachment, which is a primary requirement for quality care according to many experts. Attachment provides a sense of trust and security, but requires emotional commitment on the part of caregivers. Such commitment is way beyond the demands of most jobs. In teacher and caregiver training programs, little attention is paid to how to be empathetic, manage one's own feelings, and create caring relationships. None of the caregivers Elliot interviewed learned these skills in classes—they learned them by themselves on the job.

Relationships is a key word in this book and not just with babies. Elliot shows how the work of caregiving means involvement with families. In order for care to be consistent, caregivers and parents must work together. The idea is to harmonize the care so the baby doesn't feel a huge gap between the cultural context of the home and that of the child care setting. As Elliot says, "Maintaining their own separateness within a web of relationships proved challenging at times for the caregivers. Keeping her own values while accepting parents' values could stretch a caregiver's empathy." The key is to be your own person and support the other rather than judging. Being your own person *in relationship* means feeling a connection to others, accepting their values and beliefs but not giving up your own.

The section called "Relationship with Self" struck a particular chord in me. As Elliot's friend and colleague I have worked with her and a small group of other educators and trainers to create workshops that help early childhood education and care (ECEC) professionals make connections with the self. We call our work *Personal* Professional Development, where the idea is to help people who work with young children and their families gain: 1) self-knowledge, 2) insights about their work, and 3) an understanding of their needs at deeper levels. Through a variety of specially designed hand-on activities for self-reflection, participants in our workshops explore how to nurture and energize themselves. As a result, they report that they experience peace and calm. We think of our *Personal* Professional Development approach as a short self-improvement course to raise emotional intelligence and spiritual awakeness. Being able to deal with stress and change your emotional energy at will is one of the goals of *Personal* Professional Development. That ability serves caregivers well. As Lynn, one of Elliot's interviewees said, "the calmer you are, it tends to bring [tension in] the room down."

Both Elliot and I were appalled a few years ago to read Robin Leavitt's observations of some infant-toddler caregivers in her book *Power and Emotion in Infant-Toddler Day Care* (1994). The picture Leavitt painted was realistic and familiar to both of us. Each of us has seen just what Leavitt has observed—caregivers who treated babies and toddlers like objects instead of like people. Elliot set out to prove that all caregivers weren't like that. This book is proof. I wish that Elliot could tell us that across North America caregivers are carefully chosen and trained in the kind of caregiving she describes, but her research indicates otherwise. I wish she could tell us that the caregivers she interviewed were in situations that are typical of the field. Instead she tells us that these were exceptional programs. The general turnover rate in the average program indicates that most caregivers don't stay as long as the ones she interviewed. The state of status and salaries are two reasons for high turnover. Under-funded programs, low morale, lack of recognition for the job they do discourages many caring people from entering the field and some caregivers from remaining in it.

We're Not Robots is a wake-up call. Caregivers with the understanding, knowledge, and skills Elliot describes are the exception at present, not the norm. Elliot gives us an idea of what could be reality on a widespread basis if the field of infant-toddler care had more financial resources, could recruit potential caregivers and could train them better, including providing information and skills in self-reflection and in the art of creating human relationships. This book could change the way caregivers relate to children and parents. The first years are important years. They last a lifetime. As a society we need to be sure that all infants and toddlers who spend their days in out-of-home environments have the quality of care that this book shows is possible

—Janet Gonzalez-Mena
Fairfield, California

Chapter 1

Relationship with a Baby

Hector was under a small table hollering and holding onto the table's leg. His mother was screaming that it was time to go home and hauling on one of his legs to pull him out. I was hovering ineffectually between them. I tried to soothe the mother while explaining to Hector it was time to go home.

Two-year-old Hector enjoyed being at daycare. Each day, he happily involved himself in a project when he arrived, and he stayed involved in one project or another the entire time he was there. One morning, he worked hard to figure out how to undo the drain to the water table. He succeeded and there was water everywhere.

This particular day, he was deeply involved with the trucks.

His mother was an impatient young woman who liked to move fast. With long legs and dressed in stylish short skirts and big shoes, she was usually in a hurry to get to the next place. This day, she had plans.

I was a young teacher with idealistic notions about the care of children. I tried to keep the atmosphere in the room calm and nurturing. I tried to support parents. I cared about the children whom I cuddled, read to, chatted with, and played with every day.

That afternoon, I was not maintaining a peaceful, nurturing environment.

I cared for Hector, I empathized with his mother, and I managed to help them get out the door. I absorbed the emotional energy of Hector, his mother, and the children in the room. Afterwards, away

1

> from the children, I burst into tears. At times, the emotional tensions
> of the job were overwhelming.

More than thirty years ago, in 1972, I found myself struggling in emotionally tangled situations with no obvious course of action. Each day I was in the midst of a small group of six two-year-olds, and each day was different. I had discovered how to tune into each child and learned to manage the day, trying hard to minimize the stress on the children. Over time, I began to develop strategies for situations that arose, but some situations were more difficult than others.

Over the course of the day, all caregivers are faced with a variety of pulls on their time, emotion, and energy; they may experience the pleasure of soothing a baby, the feelings of sadness for an overwhelmed parent, or the frustration of having two crying infants at once. The tempo of the day can be hectic, peaceful, or somewhere in between, and is always unpredictable. These feelings and tensions are part of the daily life of a caregiver working with children under three in infant-toddler daycare centers. Babies need caring, nurturing, responsive relationships (Shonkoff and Phillips, 2000; Steinhauer, 1999). Hopefully they have parents and caregivers who will form such relationships with them (Gonzalez-Mena and Eyer, 1989; Shonkoff and Phillips, 2000). Establishing and maintaining a caring and responsive relationship calls for a variety of skills and calls forth myriad emotions.

The field of infant-toddler caregiving is relatively new. As Sarah Hrdy (1999, p. 506) notes, "grouping infants together...for a certain number of hours a day under the supervision of paid *alloparents*[1] who are not kin, but who are expected to act as if they are, is an evolutionary novelty, completely experimental."

This is a dramatic statement. In the past, infants have been placed together in groups, in orphanages, and with wet nurses, but infant daycare in its present form is a relatively new variation, seen only within the last sixty years.

Complexities and Nuances

I was twenty-five when I helped disengage Hector from the table leg, and I could not articulate all of the emotional tensions I experienced that day. My emotions found an outlet through my tears.

Other days in that center or, later, in other centers, I felt pulled in several directions. The dilemmas I faced were often a matter of future possibilities as well as present tensions. There was the question of whom to support: the parent, the child, or one's self, and how much support each needed, and what the results might be. At these points, endless opportunities existed to learn about relationships and one's self.

In my first years as a caregiver in the early childhood education and care (ECEC) field, I experienced a wide spectrum of emotions that I was not able to understand or articulate easily. Over time, working with babies, their families, and other caregivers, I began to clarify the array of emotions I experienced and gave voice to the complex relationships evident in so many daily events. Curious about how other caregivers handled similar situations and/or relations, I found very little scholarly work on the subject. While much attention had been given to the *subjects* of caregiving—the babies—little in the literature addressed the caregivers themselves, their attachments, and intellectual and emotional responses to their subjects. By eliciting the caregivers' perspectives I imagined contributing to a better understanding of the dynamics of caring for infants and toddlers in groups, which might lead to a better situation for both babies and caregivers.

This journey toward understanding and articulating more clearly the sometimes debilitating (Barone, 2001) tensions and creative possibilities of working with infants began in the late 1980s when I helped to set up a school-based infant daycare for young mothers (ages 19 and under) enrolled in high school, one of the first infant programs of its kind on Vancouver Island, British Columbia. The first year was busy with many challenges as I became aware of the complex emotions with which all of us were struggling, and as I wrestled with how best to support staff as their supervisor. It took the first year to get the program for the babies running well as we figured out how to respond sensitively to the needs of infants in a group. During that year, it became clear that we needed to reflect on our relationships with the young mothers who, along with their babies, needed sensitive caring as well. Finding the right balance between the relationship with the mother and the baby took skill and thoughtfulness, and dilemmas and tensions were inevitable.

When setting up the program, I investigated the concept of *primary caregiving*. Using a strategy of primary caregiving simplifies the work of caregivers while it intensifies the relationships. As a primary caregiver, each person looks after the same three infants over an extended period of time and is the main person to feed, change, and put to sleep the infants in her care. Optimally, she might care for the same infants for more than two years. Primary caregiving has been generally accepted in the field as good practice for infants and toddlers in group settings as it encourages consistency and responsiveness in the baby's relationship (Bowlby, 1978; Gerber, 1979; Gonzalez-Mena and Eyer, 1989; Lally, 1995). Together with the caregivers, I worked to establish a system of primary caregiving to fit the context of our situation.[2]

Caring for the same three babies day in, day out was an intense and intimate experience. While nestling babies close, gently changing them, feeding them, caregivers became very attached to the babies in their care. Beyond the babies and their young mothers, I found that the caregivers also needed caring support themselves, which we provided through regular and ongoing discussions. Questions and reflection were useful tools to help keep people focused on what they were doing, as well as giving them a chance to air their feelings in a safe environment and validate their experiences.

Babies, by their very nature, call forth strong emotions. There is a physical and emotional, as well as an intellectual, desire to protect and care for them (Ainsworth et al., 1978; Bowlby, 1991; Brazelton, 1983). The emotional response of a caregiver to an infant is based on her own history of attachment (Main, Kaplan, and Cassidy, 1985), her own knowledge and understanding of infants, and the meaning she brings to her work. The primatologist Sarah Hrdy says, "My children's deliciousness rendered *me* more willing to be consumed by *them*, to give up bodily resources, and in my own contemporary example, most importantly, time." While her comment comes from a parental point of view, babies' appeal to caregivers can be manifest on many levels and call forth memories and emotions.

My own history included a safe and protected childhood. I remember what it was like to be a very young child, remembering images, smells, and sensations from a two-year-old body. I enjoy seeing the world again through children's eyes, because I remember my own wonder at the world. I also remember my fears and confusions. Using my experience as a template for "good experiences for children," for years I did not question my assumptions about infants, toddlers, and their families. But when I began working with the young mothers in our school-based infant daycare, they forced me to probe my own beliefs more deeply and enlarge my own model of "a good childhood."

As my awareness of these young women's lives grew, some of their stories overwhelmed me. Within the context of each mother's story, I began to understand some of the reasons for the experiences she was creating for her baby. As graduates of the school program returned for reunion potluck suppers, I saw mothers and babies again after three to five years and realized that different experiences were not necessarily right or wrong; they were simply different, each unique.

The stresses on our staff were complex. At times, we had powerful and angry feelings about the poor maternal care we saw given to the babies. It was hard for staff to thoughtfully care for an infant during the day and see her go home to poor or negligent care. As caregivers developed relationships with the mothers and began to understand their situations better, there were shifting layers of feeling and emotions that often bumped up against each other.

I, too, felt torn between understanding the babies' needs and the sometimes-conflicting needs of the mothers. I learned, and at times had to relearn, to feel compassion for both, realizing there are no easy answers. Paramount for me was maintaining a calm environment for both children and mothers. Their lives were truly complicated. What we could offer was a peaceful, safe environment. As a supervisor, I tried to help by listening to caregivers, supporting their struggles to understand the tensions of the job while still trying to maintain a view of the bigger picture.

Early childhood educators are not necessarily prepared for the complicated work of caregiving. As a supervisor of infant-toddler caregivers as well as an instructor in early childhood education and care, I questioned how I could help support caregivers in their work. I began to feel a need to articulate some of the multiple layers I had experienced in the work of caring for babies and with which I had seen staff struggle. In order to maintain my own energy in the midst of this work, I needed to expand my thinking into new dimensions. I returned to graduate school and an opportunity to read, think, and write.

Over the next seven years I would read, reflect, and write on my own experiences, my observations over the years. I would also interview seven infant-toddler caregivers. I interviewed seven women who were passionate about their work. Each of these women had infant-toddler training and worked in a licensed center; each of them cared deeply about their work.

Beginning to Articulate the Practice

Having worked with women who were thoughtful and deeply involved in their practice, I had also observed infant-toddler caregivers who seemed thoughtless and uninvolved in their work. As an instructor for early childhood education I hoped that students would carry their initial enthusiasm and idealism into the field, but I knew how easily idealism and enthusiasm could be transformed into apathy and disinterest. Visiting programs where former students worked that provided poor care for babies was discouraging. I decided to interview caregivers who had specific infant-toddler training and experience about their engagement with their work. Wondering how they would articulate some of the difficult places of caring for infants I thought they might have some answers about issues that face people who care for young, vulnerable children.

Knowing that some of the issues facing infant-toddler caregivers had been exposed in Leavitt's book, *Power and Emotion in Infant-Toddler Day Care* (1994), I hoped to illuminate others. The issues are complicated, in part by the lack of discussion around some of the complexities surrounding the care of babies. The work is layered with emotions, beliefs, and values; babies have a variety of needs, as do their families, as do caregivers. By openly discussing the emotional issues, the places of tension, and the areas of ambiguity we can add dimension to the discussion of what constitutes good practice.

The first step for me was to listen to caregivers and I chose to listen to women who had infant-toddler training and struggled with providing excellent care to babies. I realized that I had been listening to caregivers for sometime now, and these conversations were leading me toward deeper discussions with individuals.

Listening to Caregivers

While working with young mothers and their babies in my school-based program, the center staff and I reflected on what attachment meant to us personally. Weekly, we discussed the program and any concerns or thoughts we had from the preceding week. A year and a half into the program, I sensed all of us struggling with conflicting emotions about the babies and mothers and asked if we could participate in our usual dialogue in a written form that might provide more time for reflection. We started a folder of written notes to each other on some of our reflections about the work and the issue of attachment. The writing was informal and written to be shared among us.

The folder usually went home or went on lunch break with whoever felt an urgency to write. I began the writing in this journal-dialogue with some questions and some thoughts, and, as I subsequently realized, I began my research through this informal work of conversation and journal-dialogue. The following discussion contains some of the voices in an excerpt from this journal-dialogue:

> Is there an unhealthy attachment? I certainly think there is, but how do we define it? Can we let children control the attachment? Perhaps when the child controls the attachment when he asks for you, he decides you are the person he'll rely on primarily. Can babies do that?
>
> Attachment has the ability to be freeing for a child or to be suffocating.
>
> In the old days grandmas and aunties looked after children and I'm sure children were attached to them. Are caregivers different? Is there a feeling of blood versus water?
>
> I think all of us respond from our own background of attachment, our own needs, and that seems normal to me. When do the needs of an adult interfere with the child's rights? Is it when the child becomes an object whose sole purpose is to

fulfill those needs? (Is the child seen as whole?) Is it when the adult constantly initiates the closeness or when the adult treats the child inappropriately?

Is it scary to feel so attached to a child? Are we more attached to one child rather than another and worried about fairness? We must watch our interactions with all the children. What does that mean?

To me, professionalism is the awareness of the dynamics occurring and not letting them affect the program and other children. The lovely feeling of closeness with a baby/toddler is a gift, which brings new realms of feelings, but should not get in the way of our caregiving or our relations with parents or support of the parent-child bond.

What about our own fear of detaching? A friend is leaving and gives you the cold shoulder before she leaves. Does it make your detachment easier? I would prefer to remain close and cry and hug. It feels cleaner.

We must think of the close attachments we've had. Some have been long-term, others have been short-term, but they have all enriched our lives. Does separation bring up our feelings around separation? What thoughts does everyone have?

Caregivers wrote back and forth for a while, taking the folder home to read the discussion, reflect, and then write their thoughts. One of them wrote quite eloquently about her own emotions concerning attachment and detachment, the benefits of working in a team and having daily discussions, and the opportunity for reflection that this journal afforded. Jade[3] wrote:

I'm finding reading and talking about others' views on attachment, detachment extremely helpful. I realize it's not as simple as the isolated incidents of caregiving in this center. We all come with our own attachments, detachment behaviors of our past! Healthy or unhealthy? It's what we come with and is such an emotional issue that I find it isn't clear. You *feel* so deeply and then begin to question just what is healthy or not in these feelings. Letting the child take the lead seems to me to be the key for judging healthy relationships. This calls for a constant awareness from us, the adults in the situation. Not always easy, but then growth and awareness aren't always an easy path.

> I haven't found the subject [of attachment to the children she works with] one that many people discuss, and I realize how isolated I've felt in the past when dealing with it. I really appreciate the team of individuals I work with that strive as a team to work on common goals for the healthiest way to work with children. The closeness of working in a team sure helps me to resolve issues that might take me much longer on my own. I appreciate the sensitivity of everyone when I broke down in my own individual struggle with this. To see a team effort of problem solving, a struggle we *all* deal with, is extremely beneficial. I feel that the thin line between healthy and unhealthy is becoming clearer as we all work to define it.

This dialogue was the beginning of a discussion that continued both in this form and around the table at staff meetings. At different times it was urgent, vital, and difficult. But ultimately it seemed to be extremely important to the emotional health of everyone concerned. Feelings once aroused can be powerful. These feelings of attachment to children were part of the complexity of the work where caregivers learn to balance their feelings with awareness, thought, and compassion.

To do a good job, caregivers must decide to be fully present to the relationships of caring. Being present places demands on caregivers on many levels, and the unarticulated emotions can make work in the field, in general, more complicated. The involvement of our feelings, our bodies, our minds, and our spirits can create complexities not usually discussed openly. I became aware that these deep feelings about caring for infants were not unique to our program.

Further Listening to Caregivers

In October 1992, I hosted a conference where Janet Gonzales-Mena spoke on looking at culturally sensitive approaches to infant-toddler programs. Since caregivers care for children from different cultures, she told us, caregivers must have an understanding of how culture influences our approach to babies. Developing a relationship with an infant's family can heighten cultural consciousness, and this can be done effectively within a system of primary caregiving. Since primary caregiving is the approach in which caregivers care for, change, and feed the same three or four infants from the group each day, it was a departure from traditional approaches to working with preschool children. Some conference participants had adopted this model while others had adopted a preschool model, where all teachers care for all children in the group. For infants, this latter model means that any caregiver can change a diaper or give a bottle.

During this workshop, some practitioners had concerns about this close work with infants and the discussion was heated. Participants expressed strong emotions both for and against the primary caregiving system. Advocates saw that babies benefited by becoming attached to one person and learning to communicate with that particular individual. Critics worried about the difficulty children experienced when they were "too attached to a caregiver" and then must make a transition to a new person. Each side felt strongly and articulated clearly about their position.

Within the field today, it is accepted wisdom that primary caregiving is the preferred method of caring for babies because it gives them the consistency and security of response that they need (Lally, 1995). But the 1992 conference debates indicated to me the strong feelings caregivers struggle with every day in their work with infants, despite the accepted wisdom amongst the experts. Intellectual theories don't always make sense to one's emotions.

These conference participants discussed the children's feelings, but would not discuss their own. Our emotional responses often have a personal historical basis. We live in a culture that values rationality, clear-headedness, and predictability: qualities not found in emotions, thus we may deny or overlook the emotional basis of our reactions. Attachment is seen to be less desirable than detachment, as the current child development theories describe children moving from the infantile state of attachment to the adult stage of detachment (Cannella, 1998).

From this workshop's heated discussion, I realized that caregivers needed to talk and give voice to areas that needed deeper exploration. I sensed some of the difficulties that might inhibit daycare staff and ECEC students from adopting practices that are considered optimal. Articulating these difficulties could begin a discussion about some of the concerns and anxieties caregivers experience in this work and would be useful when teaching new ECEC students. Perhaps a new model was called for, one that balanced head and heart, acknowledging the role of emotions in this work, what Greene (1990) calls the "tensions and passions."

Relationships are crucial to children's developing sense of themselves. As Pawl and St. John (1998) write, "human relationships are the foundations upon which children build their future" (p. 3). They go on to say, "meaning grows over time, built by **what** each partner in the relationship **does** . . . and also by **how** each partner in the relationship is" (p. 3). Being in relationship demands work on emotional, intuitive, physical, and rational levels, but keeping the energy alive on each of these levels is challenging at times. Finding words to articulate the competing pulls of caregiving calls for discussion and the exploration of new perspectives.

By understanding some of the complex issues with which caregivers struggle and by appreciating some of their solutions to these issues, we can further the dialogue about how to support better practice. Listening to caregivers can inform educational practices, institutional structures, and public policy. The focus up to now has been on what theoretical and practical knowledge good caregivers must have and on developing the best working circumstances. Talking about the complexities of infant-toddler care may begin to make us conscious of the deep questions inherent in caring for very young children, maybe even all children.

Chapter 2

The Pull to Attach

When I had my first baby, I already had a child. Jess was my step-daughter from my husband's first marriage and lived primarily with us. At seven years old she was used to being an only child. Disrupted by her parents' divorce, she had been uncomfortable with welcoming me so the idea of a sibling made her understandably anxious.

When my labor started, Jess went to spend the night with a friend who lived near the hospital. When David was born, we called our friend and she brought Jess to the hospital. Coming into the delivery room where we were with David, less than an hour old, Jess asked to hold him. While David had been ignoring the voices of the nurses and doctors, he heard Jess. At the sound of her voice he picked up his head, in a newborn sort of way, to look at her. His immediate and visible response to her voice was clear to us and to her; she was awestruck, and we were all moved.

Later, we realized that her head and voice would have been at his *in utero*-level. David had been hearing her voice for quite a while and he recognized it. His response to her was a powerful message of recognition and it pulled her into his orbit.

Most parents can testify to the enormous pull that their newborns exert on them. For example, Roiphe (1996, p.4), "I had given up my boundary, the wall of self, and in return had received obligation and love, a love mingled with its opposite, a love that grabbed me by the throat and has still not let me go." Over the last twenty years, observation and research have highlighted the many and varied capabilities of an infant to elicit the attention of the people around her (Brazelton and Cramer, 1990).

Needing adults to feed, clothe, and comfort them, babies have behaviors that work on their families, and others around them. When deeply connected with a baby, adults are motivated to do the things necessary to protect the baby and while in concept it may seem simple, in reality these motivations are multiple and complex.

Each adult brings his or her memories of past and present attachments, as well as cultural beliefs, to their relationship with a baby (Karen, 1994). Memories of being loved and loving provide meanings and models for current relationships. Culture constructs many of our beliefs about babies, when and how to respond to cries, whether a baby sleeps alone or with someone, how to speak to an infant. Each culture has important rules to govern responses to babies (Gonzalez-Mena and Eyer, 1989; Rogoff, 2003, 1990), and these rules and responses, which are subtle and may involve smells, touches, sounds, and gazing, are often unquestioned; to transgress them is often unthinkable. The protective instinct we have toward small children may be grounded deeply in us, but how we actualize some of our protective feelings is culturally determined (Gottlieb, 2004).

A century ago, a time with much higher mortality rates than we see now in the developed world, infants were seen as passive, incapable of much interaction. Over the last thirty years that thinking has changed and the focus has been on better understanding infants' capabilities. More recently, research has focused on the infant's relationship with caring adults and its implications for healthy development. Both the current brain research and attachment theory (see further in this chapter) have influenced the North American discussion of what constitutes good and appropriate care for babies.

While research has focused on how relationships benefit a baby, less attention is paid to the adult side of the relationship. Being in relationship with a baby impacts the adult on a physiological, psychological, and an emotional level. By paying close attention to the caregiving adult's emotions and understandings of this relationship, research would add another perspective in the care and caring for babies. Articulating these pulls validates the experience of caregivers.

Physical Impacts of Being-in-Relationship with a Baby

Poor and neglectful care has physical and physiological ramifications for a baby. Not only good nutrition, but the safety of caring relationships is important to optimal brain development (Steinhauer, 1999). Researchers have looked at the brains of children raised in the stressful environment of prolonged neglectful and abusive situations and found that under prolonged stress, chemicals may be released that can do harm to the developing brain (Perry, 2004, 1999, 1993). The hypothesis is that within a supportive relationship, babies' brains can develop without the prolonged interference of deleterious substances: caring, supportive relationships are good for babies. Bowlby, who developed a theory of attachment over fifty years ago, theorized that babies' optimal psychological development depends on the quality of their attachment to a primary caregiver, the mother. Much work has been done to elaborate on this theory, with most of the work focusing on the effects of the quality of the attachment relationship on the infant. The brain research seems to corroborate Bowlby's theory. But what happens at the other end of the attachment relationship, what happens to the adult?

As D. W. Winnicott (1987) said, "There is no such thing as a baby; there is a baby and someone" (p. xx). When we develop attachments or relationships the energy flows in two directions, so if the baby becomes attached to the caregiver then the caregiver must be attached to the baby. A caregiver holds a baby close and feels the weight of his body against her body, the baby nestles into the neck of the caregiver and they smell each other. The relationship between the two is an emotional one, a physical one, and new research indicates it is also a physiological one.

As we hold a baby close we feel, smell, hear, and see the particular qualities of that baby. We come to know her weight, her smell, and her sounds. Working with babies is particularly intimate. This closeness and intimacy creates physiological responses in the baby's body and the adult's body.

Calm and Connection

Human touch and simple physical contact can cause the release of the hormone oxytocin. Associated with breastfeeding, orgasm, birthing, and touching, oxytocin appears to be connected to feeling good and relaxed. Oxytocin influences maternal behavior and lowers blood pressure (Light et al., 2000). Levels of this hormone are related to feelings of trust and generosity; higher levels of oxytocin seem to increase people's levels of trust. Breastfeeding releases oxytocin in the mother, which gives her a feeling of contentment, while oxytocin is present in the milk, giving the infant a sense of well-being. How the hormone actually works is complicated and not well understood. Insel (2000, p. 176), writing about the neurobiology of attachment, warns that "we have just begun to realize how little we know."

Moberg suggests that oxytocin is the hormone responsible for a healing system of "calm and connection." While adrenaline is the hormone connected with fight or flight, oxytocin is the hormone that helps create feelings of calm and connectedness and allows for healing and growth. She feels that the oxytocin system is as important to our survival as our mechanism to respond to stress. It has been noted that in both men's and women's bodies that when our levels of oxytocin are high the effects of stress are offset and our bodies have a chance to restore themselves (Mobert, 2003).

The UCLA study on friendship among women found that women have an additional response to stress. The fight or flight response to high levels of adrenaline seems to be the more common response in men; women have a different response. Oxytocin is released in women under stress and this buffers the fight or flight response and encourages women to care for children and gather with other women. Oxytocin is released in both men and women, but testosterone may negate the hormone while estrogen enhances it. This engagement in relationships creates more oxytocin, which creates a calming effect (Taylor et al., 2000).

If caregivers' relationships with babies reward them with a feeling of calm and connectedness, their connections are embodied ones. Not only are caregivers' connections with the babies in their head and hearts, they feel them in their bodies. Oxytocin becomes a biochemical way of smiling or creating a loop that is good for everyone. Holding a baby can be good for the baby, and equally good for the caregiver.

One of the caregivers I interviewed, Dawn, found that massage, physical connection, was the method she intuitively used to connect with the teenaged mothers of the babies in her care. Touch can release oxytocin, creating that feeling of calm and connection. Dawn reported one of the young mothers to whom she had given a face massage saying to her, "thank you for my face"—a poignant remark.

Other hormones are probably involved in this loop. Prolactin, another hormone, is connected with parenting behaviors in many vertebrates. Even male vertebrates caring for their young have higher levels of this ancient hormone (Fleming et al., 2002; Schradin et al., 2003). Looking at research with birds, prolactin is found in higher levels while individual birds are engaged in nest-building and retrieval of scattered young (Hrdy, 1999). Higher levels of prolactin is also found in primate fathers who carry their young (Schradin et al., 2003). Human fathers with higher levels of prolactin were more alert and more positive in response to infant cries (Fleming et al., 2002).

While the physiological side of caregiving and parenting is inadequately understood, what we do know indicates that our perceptions of being in relationship with a baby are influenced on several levels. Our perceptions are based on our bodies, our emotions, and the meaning we make of babies and our relationship to them. A framework or theory constructed to explain the importance of this relationship between baby and mother/parent/significant adult is attachment theory.

Attachment Theory

Based on work done by ethologists in the 1950s, Bowlby introduced the term *attachment* to describe the mother-infant bond. He identified infant behaviors that he said were biologically based and were designed to insure the proximity of an infant's mother. This proximity of mother insured the baby's survival. Karen (1994, p. 95) states, "the formation, maintenance, and renewal of that proximity begets feelings of love, security, and joy. A lasting or untimely disruption brings on anxiety, grief, and depression." As Zeanah, Mammen, and Lieberman (1993, p. 333) say, " 'attachment' is used increasingly to refer to the 'attachment relationship,' which is the domain of the parent-child relationship involving the caregiver's provision of nurturance and of emotional availability in times of need, as well as the child's seeking of comfort when needed."

The discussions and research on this issue have continued in the years since Bowlby and his colleagues first put forth their ideas. Bowlby (1951), and later his colleague Ainsworth (1964), claimed, based on their observations, that the early relationships of a person impacted their subsequent emotional development. Their observations had convinced them that early experiences mattered, and that consistent and loving care provided the best context for an infant's development. Over fifty years ago, Bowlby (1951, p. 21) wrote, "the deprivation of mother-love in early childhood can have a far-reaching effect on the mental health and personality development of human beings."

The idea that infants actively invest in their relationships was contrary to earlier notions about babies, which focused on the notion of babies as relatively passive (Hrdy, 1999). Intrigued by the work of psychoanalysts (such as Freud and Klein) and the work of ethologists (such as Harlow), Bowlby proposed that infants, though vulnerable, came equipped with strategies to keep their caregiver nearby (Bowlby, 1951; Karen, 1994). As Hrdy (1999, p. 389) notes, "these newborns emerge immobile, unable to forage or regulate their own temperatures, defenseless and exposed to diverse dangers." Their best strategy for survival is to have someone who is willing to protect and defend them nearby.

In 1950, Bowlby had already been observing babies and children and writing about his ideas in London, when Mary Ainsworth arrived and went to work for him. In 1954, she went to Uganda and studied infants there (Ainsworth, 1962), finding the same attachment behaviors that Bowlby had been writing about in

London. Through observation in the babies' homes, she noted the evolution of the attachment behaviors from the first effort of the newborn to keep his mother or caregiver nearby to the toddlers' explorations using his mother as a secure base. She was particularly aware of the security the mother provided as key to the development of the toddler's autonomy, and it was this observation that led to her next project (Karen, 1994).

In 1963, Ainsworth moved back to the United States and began her *Baltimore Study of Mothers and Infants*. Observing infants in their home environment, she found almost all the same attachment behaviors in the American babies as she did in the Ugandan infants. For Bowlby and Ainsworth this was a further validation of the idea that attachment behaviors are biologically based and that there is a human drive to attach. Both Bowlby and Ainsworth argued that attachment will develop in the face of very little reward (Ainsworth and Bell, 1970; Ainsworth, 1964; Ainsworth, Bell, and Stayton, 1972); even abused children become "attached" to their parents.

Ainsworth continued her work by focusing on the quality of attachment between mother and child. This attachment could be characterized in terms of how secure a child was that his mother would respond to his need for her and how accurately and appropriately she responded. The type of attachment a child and mother displayed had implications for the child's development. A child with a secure sense of his mother's availability to help and support him was less anxious and more able to move out into the world (Ainsworth and Bell, 1970).

Subsequent researchers have added to and refined Bowlby's and Ainsworth's work. There has been some criticism that attachment theory does not take into account the other motivational systems or forces that shape the child. For example, Kagan claimed that people are more flexible than attachment theorists suggest, while Chess and others (Thomas and Chess, 1977; Chess, Thomas, and Birch, 1965) argued that temperament plays a significant role in children's attachment styles. Lieberman's (1993) work on toddlers added to the attachment work by suggesting that a child's temperament, what she refers to as a child's "behavioral style," can make the process of attachment more or less smooth, but she indicated that caregiver sensitivity to a child's particular attachment style can lessen difficulties for both child and caregiver.

Thomas and Chess (1977) identified nine dimensions of temperament that may influence the responses of children to situations: activity level, regularity of biological rhythms, approaching or withdrawing from a novel situation, adaptability to change, intensity of response, sensitivity to a stimulus, positive/negative mood, distractibility and perseverance in attaining a goal. In each dimension a child can rate as high or low or in between; many combinations are possible. These behavioral styles are modifiable and mutable over time and with circumstances. Lieberman (1993) writes, "Not only children have temperaments; parents do too. When the temperaments of parent and child are compatible, parents find it easier to work with the harder edges of the child's behavior.... When the parent and child are well matched in their temperament styles, it is easier to establish a partnership because each of them feels comfortable with the other's pace and emotional tone" (pp. 68–69).

It is too narrow to suggest the maternal-infant attachment is the primary and best bond. Most of the attachment research was done in a time when middle-class women in North America were predominantly at home with their children. When this research was gaining momentum after World War II, one income could support a family adequately and women were not in the labor force in great numbers. This intense focus on maternal-infant relationship might have done a disservice to mothers, with the perceived threat of compromising their attachment to their children increasing their guilt over their decision to work (Eyer, 1996, 1992). This narrow focus can also have the effect of making the other caregivers in a child's life seem unimportant. Thus the valuable work of caring for children was seen to rest squarely on the shoulders of mothers, and society has often ignored the contribution of other caregivers such as fathers, grandparents, siblings, and daycare staff.

Historically, other members of a community have cared for babies. Traditionally, women in their reproductive years were needed to contribute to the family or community well-being. Looking after babies was lighter work and often undertaken by older women, younger girls, or boys (Hrdy, 1999). Infants have long been cared for by more than one person and not just by their mother (Prochner, 2003).

Bowlby called our attention to babies and their active needs for being cared about and cared for. While the emphasis on the mother-child attachment may have been a reflection of his own time and place, and while the importance of attachment may be open for debate, attachment still is a useful concept to consider when caring for babies. Children can develop different attachment relationships with different people (Muir and Thorlaksdottir, 1992) developing, for example, a different attachment relationship with their father than with their mother and different again with their caregiver (Zimmerman and McDonald, 1995). This variety of relationships gives infants a variety of patterns to choose from, thus not limiting them to a single method of relating (Main and Weston, 1981).

A Cultural Take on Attachment

Not only do babies have different relationships with different people in their worlds, different cultures have different approaches to the care of babies. While babies are often thought of as "pre-cultural" and mothering as a "natural" process, contemporary child development theory has been based on research carried out with middle-class, Euro-American children (Gottlieb, 2004). Most of the research on infant attachment has taken place within European or American families and contexts. When researchers question these culturally bounded theories, the discussion about caring for infants becomes broader and richer (Gottlieb, 2004; Rogoff, 2003; Scheper-Hughes, 1992). No longer simply a discussion of nature versus nurture, cross-cultural research has led us to a deeper quest to understand different perspectives.

The interpretations of an infant's gurgle or cry and the appropriate responses to those signals are culturally influenced, as culture often defines who cares for the infant and under what circumstances (Rogoff, 2003). Not only who cares for the baby but how the baby is viewed and interpreted is culturally influenced. By examining other cultures and communities, other patterns of caring for infants, beyond the one most commonly described in child development texts, can be discerned. For example, the mother may not be the sole caregiver; in some communities, infants may have experience with multiple caregivers and may be encouraged to be friendly and welcoming to strangers (Rogoff, 2003). Infants may display limited stranger anxiety, unlike that described by Ainsworth, if they are encouraged from birth to interact with a wide variety of people (Gottlieb, 2004).

Challenging environments can create problems for families caring for babies. Scheper-Hughes (1992) tells of the culture that poverty and hunger in a shanty town in Brazil has created. In these shanty towns, mothers tend to neglect the babies who seem too weak to survive, calling them "angel-babies" and leaving them to starve. The women say, "There is little sorrow for the death of an infant up until the age of eight or nine months" (p. 437). This seems contrary to our culturally bound notion of "maternal instinct," but the barrio communities of Brazil have evolved explanations and strategies to help women and their families cope with the effects of the desperate poverty they experience. Even in our own society, over a hundred years ago it was quite common for babies to die (Ulrich, 1990). Contemporary historians have to research family histories carefully as the same name would be given to several babies until one survived (D. C. Elliot, personal comment).

The question of security of attachment is a particularly North American-Western European concern, where a secure attachment, usually to one person, is considered the ideal. Some cross-cultural work mentioned previously suggests that Ainsworth's "strange situation" may not be a valid method of assessing the attachment of children, as different communities may promote different qualities of attachment. Some cultures may encourage early independence while other cultures foster openness with all adults while still another might wish children to relate "properly" to adults (Rogoff, 2003). Other researchers (Posada et al., 2002) feel the key issue is "whether the link between quality of early care and infant security, not the proportion of infants in the different attachment groups, is consistent across contexts and cultures" (p. 67). Posada et al. feel their research indicates that the "relation between quality of early care and infant security holds in diverse cultural contexts" (p. 73).

Kestenberg-Amighi (2004) discussed the differences of infant-caregiver contact between North America and Bali. She found that the high-contact culture of Bali focuses children on interconnection and interdependence. Through physical contact children experience the process of separating from their mother to other family and community members noting, "Babies, handed from person to person, learn that separation from their mothers often leads to connections with others" (p. 36).

Most of the child development literature focuses on the baby and how caregiving approaches have different impacts on her growth and development. This particular focus is symptomatic of a particular North American positivist approach. Cause and effect thinking surrounds this research and motivates our interest in it. Underlying this discussion of secure attachment and its benefits for the child is the belief that if we can be a certain "right way," a child will turn out well. Scientific methods have given us a false sense of being in control of the outcome. Developing an assembly line to produce efficient cars is different than producing the perfect baby. Scientific methods have been successful at creating material success so it is hard to resist thinking that it can work in producing the right type of human being.

Hoping to ask the right questions in order to discover the formula to successful child rearing, we focus on babies and what is happening with them. They become the problem we are trying to solve. There is an illusion that it is within our power to mold babies to become the right type of person. This becomes a problem when this approach is considered universal or appropriate for everyone.

With all the focus on the baby we often neglect the caregiver experience, with the exception of mothering. There is a cultural tendency to encourage mothers to follow certain prescriptions to create a certain type of child, and if the child does not turn out to fit the mold, we then blame the mother. Non-maternal caregivers, or alloparents, are ignored except for how they respond to the infant.

In the discussion of care for infants and toddlers outside of the home, caregivers are told to be developmentally appropriate, sensitive, and responsive to the children in their care (Bredekamp and Copple, 1997). A formula or a specific model does not guide the process of entering into a relationship with a baby and his or her family; it is a highly individual and unique process. As one of the participants of this study clearly said, "We're not robots."

A baby learns to relate to her particular family and community, discovering that different people will be comforting and different situations will arouse anxiety. Babies learn whom to turn to for comfort, whom to listen to respectfully, whom to play with, and these will differ by culture and family. For their survival, infants must depend on their family and their community. Whiting and Edwards (1998) speak of the role of intuition and empathy in the caring for a baby or toddler: "It is also important in considering the stereotypes of male and female behavior to remember that training in nurturance to nonverbal humans is training in intuition, a trait that, according to Western stereotypes, is considered to be characteristic of females. The caretaker of the pre-verbal child must guess the needs and wants of someone who cannot communicate by speech. Being able to intuit the child's desires requires that the individual draw on empathy, consciousness of her own wants in similar situations, or previous experience" (pp. 181–182). This "consciousness" depends on many elements in the caregiver's history, beliefs, and understanding of herself.

The literature on child development is now moving beyond the polarizing discussion of nature versus nurture to a richer discussion of the interplay of forces within relationships. Children and adults learn about each other and the world through their bodies, spirits, emotions, and intellect. The interplay is multidimensional.

Brain Research and Attachment

During the past twenty years, research on the brain and its development in the early years of childhood has implicated the role of early experiences in children's development (Shonkoff and Phillips, 2000); early experiences have an impact on the wiring of the brain in the first year or two. This research has raised public awareness and has implications for infant care.

Research suggests that the brain continues to develop after birth and its development can be harmed by severe stress. Perry (1993) found that the cortical and subcortical areas of the brains of children who had been severely neglected and abused had not developed properly and were roughly 20 to 30 percent smaller than normal. His findings suggest that this underdevelopment can affect intelligence and emotional health. A *New Yorker* article quoted Perry as saying, "If early in life you are not touched and held and given all the somatosensory stimuli that are associated with what we call love, that part of the brain is not organized in the same way" (Gladwell, 1997, p. 140). Other research suggests that continual high levels of stress hormones (e.g., cortisol) are harmful to the developing brain (Gunnar et al., 1996).

Brain research has been cited by those aware of the urgency of providing good care to infants. Hertzman (2000), for example, argues that, "spending one's early years in an unstimulating, emotionally and physically unsupportive environment will affect brain development in adverse ways" (p. 14). Marcus, Vijayan, Rao, and Vishton (1999), Newberger (1997), and Steinhauer (1999) all echo the warnings that the experiences of the first year of life will affect the child's later life and abilities. Chronic maltreatment experiences can have long-term effects on children, such as lower IQ scores, depression, behavioral difficulties, and emotional problems (Shonkoff and Phillips, 2000). Steinhauer (1999) describes one possible effect of chronic maltreatment: a disruption in regulation of feelings, followed by increased arousal and leading to a lack of empathy for others. Brain researchers consistently point to the importance of paying attention to the *quality* of experience that is provided for babies, because what seems to cushion children's experiences at a young age is the quality of their relationships with significant adults (Fancourt, 2000). Newberger (1997) wrote, "Positive interactions with caring adults stimulate a child's brain profoundly, causing synapses to grow and existing connections to be strengthened" (p. 6). As well, a positive attachment can be effective in mediating the infant's stress levels (Shonkoff and Phillips, 2000). A good quality of attachment to a significant adult can provide internal mediation of the events of early life.

While the current findings about brain growth bolsters the case for promoting the quality of care for infants, there has been criticism of the way the current brain research has been used by the child advocacy field. Bruer (1999), in *The Myth of the First Three Years*, points out that the influence of the first three years' experience on the development of brain circuitry is not yet clear. He is concerned that recent findings about the brain have created a "myth" concerning the lasting impact of the first three years.

While the brain does continue to develop after birth, he argues, it is not known how and to what extent the environment affects that growth. "The myth's popularity and its beguiling, intuitive appeal is rooted in our fascination with the mind-brain, and our perennial need to find reassuring answers to troubling questions" (p. 27). Some of the work done by Ames, Chisholm, and their associates with Romanian orphans who endured very poor care in the first months and years of their lives has also called into question some of the "urgency" of the first three years. A number of those children adopted into Canadian families have been able to form positive attachments after the theoretically optimal age of one or two years old, and their developmental lag in a number of areas has decreased over time (Chisholm et al., 1995; Chisholm, 1995). However, if the adoption happened before the child was eight months old, minimal developmental lags and secure attachments with the adoptive parents were more likely (Ames, 1997).

While the controversy continues, it is evident that children still need the provision of consistent emotional and physical support for optimal development. As Brandt (1999) suggests, "information from brain research cannot provide definitive answers... but combined with what we already know, it can add to our understanding" (p. 237). Whether we provide good care for babies because it will make their brains brighter or because they have a right to be appreciated for who they are, the brain research adds another dimension to our consideration of the supports babies need.

Feeling Pulled by Babies

Attentive caregiving benefits babies, and giving care at this level demands that caregivers that they are involved on a physical, emotional, and intellectual level. Emotions play a large role in relationships and thus in the work of an infant-toddler caregiver. How do caregivers handle the emotional dimensions of the job, in particular, the emotional tensions? The feelings of warmth and closeness we feel with infants are easier to talk and think about than the feelings of anger, resentment, and frustration one may also feel. Emotions can and do drive action and at times, they can override one's formal knowledge and understanding of good infant care. Feelings are very powerful, even overwhelming. Behavior may be easy to define, but the emotional and spiritual side of caring is, as Goldstein (1997, p. 8) says, "mushy, fuzzy, subjective, personal, loaded."

Quantifying the feeling side of caregiving may not be possible, but we can ask the women who care for other people's babies about their "mushy, fuzzy" experiences of caregiving. Leavitt's powerful study deconstructs the infant-toddler programs she visits in terms of the use of power and emotion and gives us a picture of what happens when caregivers take the option to stay emotionally uninvolved in their work. She acknowledges that caregivers are "significant emotional associates in children's lives" (p. 2), but her observations of caregivers and their interactions with babies are discouragingly negative. The care she saw was unresponsive and dismissive. The women involved in the caregiving appeared to have avoided and denied the emotional aspect of caring, and in doing so have denied the babies in their care an emotionally rich environment. However, Leavitt says that her work did not include the caregivers' perspective, as her work was based on her observations and she did not speak with the caregivers. Nonetheless, Leavitt demonstrated that caregivers can choose not to put their heart into their jobs, and we can only wonder why.

Elements of good practice are discussed in the next chapter. Good practice asks caregivers to enter into meaningful relationships with children and their families. To stay engaged with the children and families in their care these women must stay alert to the nuances of their relationships.

Chapter 3

Caring for Attachment

Ashley was four months old and a beautiful baby. Round and dim-
pled at knees and elbows, she smiled and responded happily to
people. It was a pleasure to be in her company. One afternoon on a
warm autumn day I was sitting beside her and enjoying the warmth
and peace of that moment. I heard Ashley's father come in. He was
a medium size young man with a well-developed set of muscles. He
was aware of them, as were all of us; even on chilly days he wore a
sleeveless undershirt. There was an air of danger about him and we
could sense the potential violence in him.

Ashley had also heard her father. I observed her as she got
ready to see him. She pulled in her head and pulled in her arms
and legs so that she was a compact bundle. She had already learned
that was the most comfortable and safest way to be picked up by
her father. He arrived and with an energetic swoop swung her in
the air unmindful of supporting her head. She had already done
what she could to protect herself against his exuberance.

Caregivers have to struggle with the "tensions and passions"
of their daily practice (Greene 1990). These tensions and
passions have no easy resolution, but naming and talking about
them make them easier to embrace and as they are faced, lessons
can be learned from them. We all know there are emotional
rewards as well as dangers within relationships. As Suzanne
Gordon (1996, p. 185) says, "We oddly refuse to allow others to

learn that sanity does not lie in the path of detachment, but can also abound on journeys of the most intimate, personal and emotional discovery."

The complex emotional pulls of the work of teachers, nurses, doctors, social workers, infant-toddler and preschool caregivers are not often discussed. Many professional groups have guidelines to regulate professionals' behavior in order to prevent individuals from experiencing difficult emotional situations or ethically compromising positions. One such guideline indicates that one should not get "involved" with the people with whom one works (Registered Nurses Association of British Columbia, n.d.). Benner and Wrubel (1989) call this "controlled caring." But working in a relationship with babies and families requires involvement and an emotional commitment, and that commitment can go beyond "control."

For too long we have worked under the idea that relational work can be governed by rules and regulations. This mechanistic approach to caregiving flattens the work, giving the impression of a collection of simple behaviors and tasks. The process of caregiving is far too complex, multidimensional, and important to continue with this notion.

When a baby brightens at the sight of her special person and starts to chortle as that person gets closer and then bursts into a big smile when picked up, that person does indeed feel special (and all those chemicals have started to dance in her body!). The adult becomes attached to the baby and responds to the baby's emotions with emotions of her own. The engagement is mutual. As Benner and Wrubel (1989) write, "Involvement and caring may lead one to experience loss and pain, but they also make joy and fulfillment possible" (p. 3).

Three teachers of infants and toddlers, Rowe, Early, and Loubier (1994), have written: "While the demands are high, the rewards are plentiful. It never grows old to see a child take his first step or hear him put together initial sentences. The intensity of the child-teacher relationship is professionally unparalleled. While these children require us to reach deep down and share ourselves physically and emotionally, they reciprocate with smiles, hugs, and by sharing a never-ending stream of thrilling accomplishments" (p. 28).

Daycare for Babies?

What does the current research say about daycare for infants? In the previous chapter, I have asserted that the care a baby receives is important for the development of a good foundation from which to move into childhood. Twenty years ago, there was a great deal of caution in recommending daycare for babies (Belsky and Rovine, 1988). At the present time it is commonly agreed that daycare is a positive option *if* it is of high caliber (Vleveland and Krashinsky, 1998; Doherty, 1999, 1999a). As Palacio-Quintin says, (2000, p. 17) "the initial question, a simple and sometimes biased one, was whether attending daycare had a negative impact on children. We have moved on to a more objective and complex set of questions."

Palacio-Quintin (2000, p. 20) sums up the characteristics of quality daycare, in general, as "a qualified and stable staff, a good educational program, good teacher-child and parent-daycare relationships, groups that are not too big, a reasonable amount of safe space, and safe hygiene practices." Warm and sensitive care and quality interactions promote secure attachment. Howes, Phillips, and Whitebrook (1992) describe an engaged type of caregiving they call "involved teaching," which asks for high levels of touching, hugging, talking, and engagement between baby and caregiver.

Caregivers must respond sensitively to each baby, getting to know that particular baby's signals and cues (Elliot, 1995; Fein, Garibaldi, and Boni, 1993; Howes and Hamilton, 1993; Howes and Smith, 1995). Brazelton and Kagan among other child psychologists and researchers, (Brazelton and Cramer, 1990; Brazelton, Koslowski, and Main, 1974; Kagan, 1978, 1984, have drawn the public's awareness to the individual differences that can be seen in newborns. Lally (1995) cautioned that infants are "evolving individual identity" (p. 67) and went on to say that infant-toddler caregivers "participate either knowingly or unknowingly in the creation of a sense of self and that attention must be paid to that unique responsibility" (p. 67). Evolving from an infant's relationship with others is his or her sense of agency. It takes great care and thought to respond to each child's style and family context so that the infant develops a secure sense of self.

This debate should be situated in its historical and cultural context. There have always been "alloparents" (Hrdy, 1999). The debate about child care's suitability for infants makes it appear as if it is a new social experiment, but communities and nonmaternal individuals across all cultures have looked after children for centuries (Gottlieb, 2004; Rogoff, 2003). With the evolution of industry and cities, we live in increasingly larger groups, and communities must redefine themselves and the role they will play in children's lives (Prochner, 1996).

Given good care babies thrive with their parents, with relatives, with other caregivers. Good care can perhaps be a way to enhance vulnerable children's chances for success in later life. This is the premise of many programs that were developed over the last century (Prochner, 1996).

Care for Resilience

In the early seventies, when I was helping Hector let go of the table leg (chapter 1), I was working in New York City at the Infant Care Unit of the Jewish Board of Guardians, a program begun by the psychiatrist Roy Lillesov (Resch et al., 1977). Lillesov had been a psychiatrist for enough years to see a pattern among his patients, some of whom coped with life better than he would have predicted given their painful and difficult childhood. He began to realize those "successful" patients each had a warm and caring person to whom they had related in their early years. Lillesov's infant care unit, situated in a low-cost housing project, was set up for infants and toddlers living in high-stress situations. The unit provided psychiatrists and social workers to work with families, while a warm and supportive child care program was provided for the children.

Reaching children in the early years has been one method used in North America to help support and assimilate immigrant, poor, and/or "at risk" children. In the 1880s, preschool programs, essentially programs of assimilation, were designed to help immigrant children adjust to life in the United States and Canada (Mayfield, 2001). In the early days of day nurseries and preschools, quality of care focused on ensuring the children's health and safety (Prochner,

1996). Today, in Canada, there have been compensatory programs for children at risk, such as the Aboriginal Headstart program and the CAP-C (Community Action Program for Children), which offer preschool programs to specially designated groups of children (Beach, Bertrand, and Cleveland, 1998). The recent trend is to aim compensatory programs at "school-readiness."

While Lillesov had made his observations on a small and personal scale, Emmy Werner (1987; Werner and Smith, 1982) did research looking at some of the factors that seemed to protect people from difficult life circumstances. On Kauai, Hawaii, Werner began a longitudinal study of over 600 children born in 1955. Over the years she monitored these children, documenting health, education, and social status at ages 1, 2, 10, and 18 years and then ages 30 to 32 years old. One in three children in the cohort were deemed at risk because there was some perinatal stress; they were either born into poverty, had mothers with little formal education, or lived in a family situation that was unstable because of alcoholism, violence, and/or mental illness. In this group of at risk children were many who developed behavioral problems or learning problems, but one in four of these children developed into competent, caring adults. Looking more closely at these *resilient* children, Werner found that some of the buffering factors were a child's own sociability, a warm emotional support system with a parent, sibling, grandparent, neighbor, or teacher, and informal support systems at school, work, or church that rewarded an individual's sense of competence and provided a sense of meaning. A warm and caring adult had supported such a child, and it seemed as if the first year of life was particularly important to future development.

From the brain development perspective, Bruce Perry found that traumatic events had less of a detrimental effect on a child's developing brain if a child had a supportive and nurturing family. Having nurturance and security seems to protect brain development as well as provide emotional support.

Good Practice

There has been a growing need and demand in North America for more daycare facilities. Many families need two incomes and women are increasingly working outside the home. The population is more mobile than in the early and middle part of the twentieth century, and care for children is no longer typically the responsibility of an elder member of the family or older siblings. Children are increasingly cared for outside the home, resulting in an increase in programs designed to care for children and/or enhance children's development (Beach et al., 2004; Hofferth, 1992).

What we are learning about early development has contributed a sense of urgency to the work of those designing and implementing programs for families and babies considered at risk (Lally and Keith, 1997; Mann, 1997). Emerging research and knowledge about brain development has added fuel to the concerns of parents who want to enrich their children's environments to optimize their development.

The debate about the elements of good care for children has been ongoing (Doherty 1999; Phillips 1987). Palacio-Quintin (2000) looked at almost 200 studies that examine the issue of how daycare affects the development of children, newborn to 6 years old, and found that daycare centers appear to be more beneficial than family daycare facilities. She goes on to say that the quality of the daycare center "plays a primary role in child development" (p. 21). She advocates for "teacher training and stability and, consequently, their working conditions must be top priorities, as well as high-quality educational programs. The parents' relationship with the daycare and communication between parents and teacher are other key factors in quality care. Maintaining good sanitary conditions and providing physical resources also contribute to the children's proper development" (p. 21).

Experts at the National Center for Infants, Toddlers, and Families (Lally et al., 1995) state that quality care for infants in centers rests on the following components within the child care setting: promotion of health and safety, small group size, high staff-to-child ratio, providing a primary caregiver for each child, continuity of care, responsive caregiving with individualized planning, cultural and linguistic sensitivity, and a stimulating physical environment. But good care for infants and toddlers is not only defined by group size and ratios, but also by the experience and training of the teachers involved (Clarke-Stewart, 1992; Howes and Hamilton, 1993). For example, staff who have college degrees were more sensitive and appropriate in their responses to the children in their care than were caregivers with less education. Caregivers with more years of experience were more likely to provide more responsive caregiving (Whitebrook, Howes, and Phillips, 1990).

Another component critical to good practice is the way in which caregivers work with parents. Demonstrating respect and meeting parents' needs has been accepted as part of an infant-toddler teacher's job (Doherty, 1999; Hamilton, 1994; Rowe, Early, and Loubier, 1994). Lally (1995) says, "patterns of care should give the child a sense of connection with the home and, more importantly, communicate that where she comes from is respected and appreciated" (p. 65). The hope is that when caregivers and parents are working together, the infant will feel the harmony and the resulting care may be more consistent between home and childcare setting.

Although the largest body of childcare research has been done in the United States, there have been Canadian studies. For example, Goelman and Pence (1987) have studied differing types of daycare and the effects on children's language. In the Canadian National Child Care Study (Lero et al., 1992), the child care situation is discussed. Though the two countries are similar, Howe and Jacobs (1995, p. 138) remind us there are national differences that must be considered: "The Canadian perspective is more oriented towards social assistance than the American." They go on to say that, overall, the licensing standards are higher in Canada.

There has been criticism of the indicators used to define quality care for children. The idea that criteria developed within a North American or European culture can be generalized to encompass notions of quality in all cultural contexts is called into question (Benner, 1999; Penn, 1999). This is an important concern and sensitizes us to approach programs with appreciation for the context and culture of each setting and another reminder that this work takes thought and skill. With this in mind, small groups and caring, responsive practitioners are an essential bottom line for infant-toddler programs and are more likely to be responsive to context and culture. How to create the possibility for attachment between caregiver and baby appears to be a key consideration.

Primary Caregiving

There is an increasing trend over the last fifteen years to a primary care model for infants, a system in which an infant is attended to by one person rather than several. Primary caregiving is not a recent idea. Provence (1974), for example, mentions primary caregivers in her description of her daycare program for children under the age of 2 at the Yale Child Study Center. She stated, "We gave each child a primary caregiver... because of the stability of our staff—there was very little turnover—it worked out that the children came to know all of the child care staff very well. Nevertheless, to have the person who knew him best available through most of the day was important for obvious reasons, making him more secure and comfortable" (p. 11).

More recently, others have associated primary caregiving with good practice (Lally et al., 1995; Lally and Keith, 1997). Advocates of primary caregiving, Lally et al. (1995, p. 64) wrote, "when the separation-individuation process is considered as an important component of the child care experience, it makes great sense to limit the number of caregivers with whom a child must interact each day and to structure his experience so that it is easy for him to form an intimate relationship with a known and trusted adult. This is best done by assigning a primary caregiver to each child."

In a further description of primary caregiving, Bernhardt (2000, p. 74) wrote, "In the primary caregiving model, each caregiver or teacher within a larger group is assigned primary responsibility for a specific group of children. For example, in an infant care room with a ratio of three to one that serves 12 babies, each caregiver is responsible for the care of the same three children every day. This does not mean the caregiver cares exclusively for the same three children; rather, that she has principal responsibility for the few children in her direct care."

Bernhardt's statement describes a system that meets the goals of providing responsive, consistent care. This system requires that staff work as a team and communicate closely about the working day. As Lee (2000, p. 14) remarks, "the practical application of this philosophy into a center does require thought and planning." Bernhardt discussed the importance of primary caregiving and says, "although primary caregiving has caught on across the country—and experts on quality care issues often imply a primary caregiving system or even mention it by name in their writing" (p. 74), not everyone understands the model.

The questions of how to best provide care for babies outside the home arose as the need for daycare increased. Primary caregiving became a practical model for offering consistency of care for infants, care that fits their needs for an individual, responsive, warm relationship with an individual caregiver. Gonzalez-Mena and Eyer in their fifth edition of *Infants, Toddlers, and Caregivers*, state that "a primary caregiving system doesn't solve all attachment issues, but it makes a big step toward addressing them" (p. 45).

An early proponent of primary caregiving was the Hungarian pediatrician Emmi Pikler, who began her work in the 1930s. Pikler, aware of the ideas of Bowlby and his colleagues and aware of the psychoanalytical trends of the time, began to develop her ideas of respecting infants and their innate abilities. In her work with parents and babies, she emphasized the autonomy of the infant. She believed young children to be competent and believed infancy to be a stage of life with experiences as vital and meaningful as those of adults (Penn, 1999).

Pikler became the director of the Loczy Institute, an orphanage in Budapest. Concerned about the results of observational studies that pointed to poor development among children living in orphanages, Pikler believed she could devise a system that respected the needs of the babies. She wrote, "the infant still needs an intimate, stable, adult relationship, and that is the leading principle of infant care and education as practiced at Loczy" (Pikler, 1979, p. 90). She also believed that "a satisfactory relationship between adult and child is formed primarily during the physical contacts, i.e., dressing, bathing, feeding, etc., when the adult and child are in intimate personal contact" (pp. 90–91).

Magda Gerber trained with Pikler and brought her ideas to the United States when she fled Hungary after the revolution in 1956. Through her work with parents and infants, she set up a program called Resources for Infant Educarers (RIE). Like Pikler, Gerber had a philosophy of respecting babies and recognizing their many abilities, believing that having a consistent, or primary, caregiver promotes security in the child. She (Gerber and Johnson, 1998, p. xiv) wrote, "A carer puts love into action. The way you care for your baby is how he experiences your love. Everyday caregiving routines, like feeding and diapering, can be educational and loving interactions....Allowing infants to learn on their own rather than actively stimulating or teaching them is a basic RIE tenet. Children learn all the time, from the day they are born. If we refrain from teaching them, they learn from experience."

All of the caregivers I interviewed had experience with Magda and RIE. Lynn had taken a two-week course, RIE 1, with Gerber and was impressed with her. She said, "the way she talks about it;...it's her life. She shares what is so important for her with you that infants are such capable individuals she brings it alive for you."

In North America, the primary caregiver system has focused on the caregiver and infant, rather than on the infant and environment or infant and peers. While Pikler did encourage caregivers to remain with their infants to maintain consistency, she felt the whole environment should be constant and predictable; she felt that babies must have "freedom for activity and adequate space. Their environment must be stable, varied and colorful" (Pikler, 1979, p. 91). In that sense, she was anticipating research that later demonstrated that children become attached not only to their caregiver but to the physical surroundings and the other children as well (Whaley and Rubenstein, 1994). Pikler (1979) was also clear that the infants should be active participants in their relationships with the world and their caregivers.

Yet not everyone agrees with this model. Wright (2001), for example, warned about the exclusivity of a primary caregiver model. Urging practitioners in the field to critically question their position on primary caregiving, he says, "the exclusive use of the term 'primary caregiver' means that any alternative interpretation of that term becomes suspect. It becomes impossible to reframe, reconstruct or reinvent early childhood programs except in light of that exclusivity" (p. 18). This is an important reminder for caregivers, and it speaks of possible tensions in the practice of primary caregiving.

Primary caregiving is a commitment to developing in-depth relationships with a baby and that baby's family. Staff do not always welcome this in-depth manner of working with children; working this intimately with a child and family can arouse fears.

Staff may fear that there may be a baby they will not like or that a child will get "too attached" to a staff member and not accept other staff people. During the interviews conducted for this study, all of the caregivers had some experience with primary caregiving. I asked them how they felt about it and the responses were positive. As Rachel said, "It completely changed the program, it changed relationships with staff, with parents, everything."

Chapter 4

The Public Story of Caregiving

Negotiating for better staff salaries as director of a child care program, I told the funding agency representative the following story as part of my case that the child care staff's care of the toddlers was therapeutic.

> We were having a hard time with eighteen-month-old Jim. He arrived each morning and started emptying shelves and throwing toys. Once he had emptied the shelves, he turned his attention to the smaller toddlers and began to push, systematically, them all over. As our oldest toddler, he was also the biggest and a push from him could send some of the slighter babies flying.
>
> Jim was a sturdy boy and he had been in our program for more than a year. We had seen him grow from a round, smiling infant to a big toddler, comfortable with our environment and with us. His mother, Danielle, was very shy and we had taken a year to establish a relationship with her. For the first few months, she had said almost nothing to any of us. After awhile she started hanging around more and chatting. She was in a somewhat unsettled and, at times, volatile relationship.
>
> These types of relationships and toddlers don't always mix. We knew that things at home were difficult for Jim as his strivings for independence ran headlong into the young couple's need for his compliance. Their skills in coping with his energy and with his increasing sense of self were minimal.

We tried our usual tactics of engaging him in an activity when he arrived in the morning, anticipating his assaults on the younger children and intervening; but we were not making much headway. Jim talked very little and, of course, a toddler does not have the concepts, let alone the words, needed to explain what is bothering him.

As adults, when we are upset, we need to have someone present for us who is trying to understand the confusions and dilemmas that life presents. As J. A. Kottler (1993) says in his book *On Being a Therapist*, "This healing relationship between people goes beyond mere catharsis: human beings have an intense craving, often unfulfilled, to be understood by someone else" (p. 8). Toddlers want to be understood, too. We decided to pay attention and to be present to what Jim wanted to tell us about his life.

We organized our schedule so that when Jim arrived, his caregiver, Martha, met him at the door and took him to a small room where there were a few toys and pillows. The other care-givers managed the rest of the children as Martha took time to be with Jim and "listen" to what he had to tell her. It was a "therapy" session without the words, but with an attitude of attention on Martha's part. Being present for another can happen on many levels. Here, Jim could empty shelves, throw pillows, and stomp around the room without endangering the other children. Martha spoke to him about what she was experiencing with him. After half an hour or so, Jim returned to the group ready to join in.

What Kottler goes on to say is true of work with infants: "Intimacy means being open, unguarded, and close to another. To facilitate trust, the therapist must feel comfortable facing intimacy without fear. This closeness helps the client to feel understood and appreciated; it teaches him that true intimacy is indeed possible, that a relationship based on regard and respect is desirable" (p.44). Martha was able to accept the feelings that Jim expressed through his body and be ready for him when he needed finally to connect and be reassured.

The administrator listened patiently and was supportive but said the time was not right, that the other administrators wouldn't "buy it" as a rationale for paying daycare staff higher wages to bring them into line with other counselors. While those adminis-trators refused to see and understand the value of caring work with toddlers, it is necessary to continue to articulate the work of being with and attending to babies and toddlers in order to make the knowledge and expertise of committed caregivers visible.

The skill and thoughtfulness needed to work with very young children and their families is clearly not recognized by the larger society. Listening to the infant-toddler caregivers with whom I spoke, the complexity of their work is made clear. As Doherty (2001) noted, "this perception of lack of recognition of the skills required for and high level of responsibility associated with providing child care contributes to poor morale" (p. 23). In our society, money is often equated with the value we place on a job and childcare is not a highly remunerated profession, but the real issue here is the need for recognition of the valuable contribution that caregivers make in our society.

Caregiving: A Theoretical Framework

Defining the role of an infant-toddler caregiver includes far more than a list of correct behaviors. Picking up and holding the baby can be one important behavior, but holding a baby can be done in many different ways and with different intentions. How do we perceive and describe the type of holding each baby would like? Each baby has an individual set of preferences, and a good caregiver must work this out with each baby. How a caregiver interprets the baby's signals and discovers those preferences is part of the skill she brings to the job, responding as she holds a baby and sensing a corresponding response. This job cannot be done mechanically. As Sheryl says, "you have to open a little. You can't just change a diaper with no feeling...we're not robots."

Each caregiver will approach her practice from her own internalized history, her experience as a caregiver, and from her sensitivity and responsiveness to the infant in her care, and thus a unique relationship can develop. Speaking from over ten years' experience working with young children, Jade acknowledges her skill is based on "experience, accumulated over the years. It sits there and I can probably tap into more of my intuition based on accumulated experience than I could have at one time."

Gerber (1979, p. 21) talked of paying attention to the babies we look after: "It is full, unhurried attention. Under the right circumstances it is a peaceful, rewarding time for *both* parties because, ideally, it is a time of no ambivalence, one for open listening, taking in the other person, trying to fully understand the other's point of view." This attentive presence helps caregivers find a path to relationship. One infant-toddler caregiver, Lynn, spoke of taking "the time to sit back and see what [babies] are learning... they are very capable. I watched a little fifteen-month-old snapping her fingers today. I can't even snap my fingers, and she is standing there and she is snapping them."

Within the last twenty years, the concept of an *ethic of caring* has been articulated by several authors (Benner and Gordon, 1996; Benner and Wrubel, 1989; Bowden, 1997; Calhoun, 1992; Cole and Coultrap-McQuin, 1992; Gilligan, 1982; Noddings, 1984; Ruddick, 1989). An ethic of care "is not a system of principles, rules or universalizable maxims; instead, it is a mode of human responsiveness that is manifest in particular situations and types of relationships" (Cole and Coultrap-McQuin, 1992, p. 4). As we look more closely at the work of caring and connecting with others, the complexity of the practice of caregiving becomes visible. As Bowden (1997, pp. 3–4) wrote, "understanding is directed towards consideration of the particularity of concrete situations, and their complex interconnections in the fabric of their unique participants' lives."

An ethic of care is in contrast to an ethic of justice. Gilligan's (1982) work challenged the dominant moral framework of justice that claimed morality was ruled by a set of objective universal principles (Kohlberg, 1971, 1981). Noting from the interviews conducted while working with Kohlberg that girls approached the solutions to the moral dilemmas differently than did boys, Gilligan proposed that a morality based on values found in personal relationship was equally relevant. In Gilligan's scheme of morality, the concept of identity expands to include the experience of interconnection. Through interaction, one learns that we are all related and connected. Without the opportunity and ability to learn this, our morality may remain at the level of pure formality where we may care *for* something, but not really care *about* it. Gilligan (1982) wrote, "the ethic of care develops through relationships that give rise to an understanding of interdependence and is sustained by the ability to discern connection" (p. 46). The moral domain is similarly enlarged by the inclusion of responsibility and care in relationships. "While an ethic of justice proceeds from the premise of equality—that everyone should be treated the same—an ethic of care rests on the premise of nonviolence—that no one should be hurt" (p. 173).

Margaret Walker wrote that "there are alternatives to the abstract, authoritarian, impersonal, universalist view of moral consciousness." The ethic of justice has been the prevailing voice amongst the theories of moral development: the ethic of care modifies and expands that voice, providing an alternative framework. The ethic of justice claims objectivity while an ethic of care is relative, based on context and relationship. The caring perspective "reasons" within a relational framework. Waerness called for a "rationality of caring" that draws on *both* reason and emotion to inform the practice. Caregivers need to be both conscious *and* feeling so that, for example, knowing about the nutritional needs of an infant must be coupled with an emotional responsiveness to feeding and caring for the baby.

Sarah Ruddick (1989) acknowledged the different energies that comprise the work of mothering. She says that maternal thinking requires "a unity of reflection, judgment, and emotion" (p. 214). Expanding on the discussion of caring, she looked at maternal caring, stating, "Rather than separating reason from feeling, mothering makes reflective feeling one of the most difficult attainments of reason. In protective work, feeling, thinking, and action are conceptually linked; feelings demand reflection, which is in turn tested by action, which is in turn tested by the feelings it provokes. Thoughtful feeling, passionate thought, and protective acts together test, even as they reveal, the effectiveness of preservative love" (1989, p. 70).

This discussion is being echoed in related fields; educator Nel Noddings speaks to this theme. She maintains that it is within caring relationships that we learn, and that education itself is about relationship—with each other, with ideas, with the world, and with oneself. She writes that "while much of what goes on in caring is rational and carefully thought out, the basic relationship is not, and neither is the required awareness of relatedness" (1996, p. 23).

From the field of sociology, Arlie Hochschild (1983) asked about the price that is extracted from women who are paid for "emotional work." Her study of flight attendants questions the commercialization of behaviors and emotions that were traditionally part of the private realm of experience. Her ideas about "emotional work" can be expanded and modified as we look at the work that infant caregivers do. Flight attendants, for example, do not form relationships with many passengers; infant-toddler caregivers do. While there is reciprocity in the caregiver-infant relationship that is lacking in flight attendant or host work, both flight attendants and caregivers are paid and must take responsibility for their emotions in their work.

Nelson (1990) picked up on Hochschild's ideas in her discussion of family daycare providers, who do the work of mothers and are paid to care for and about children. Unlike flight attendants who must manage their emotions, family daycare providers develop relationships with the children and families with whom they work; their emotions are engaged. And using Hochschild's term "emotional work," Cheshire Calhoun (1992, p. 118) wrote, "'Emotional work' names the management of *others'* emotions—soothing tempers, boosting confidence, fueling pride, preventing frictions, and mending ego wounds. Taking care of others, creating domestic harmony, and caring about how others fare morally calls for work on others' emotions. This emotional work eludes moral thinking. It falls outside our paradigms for moral activity." This work, which involves empathic feeling and thinking, immediacy, and reflection, is complex, and I would add that "emotional work" also involves the emotions of the caregiver. To be effective at responding to others' emotions, a caregiver must be aware of and in tune with her own emotions, in order to build a genuine relationship with a baby and parent.

These discussions of caring resonate in other fields. Nursing, for example, has included *caring* in its discourse. Building on Dreyfus and Dreyfus's (1985) work, Benner and Wrubel (1989, p. 1) say that caring "as a word for being connected and having things matter works well because it fuses thought, feeling and action—knowing and being." They feel that a mechanistic view of caring behavior is inadequate for understanding and explaining expert practice. Caring, to them, is "specific and relational." In another study examining nurses' perspectives of a quality work environment, Attridge and Callahan (1987) note that emotional support is an important requirement for nurses. The support "provides reward, value, respect and caring to professionals who, working in difficult and demanding work situations... badly require it" (p. 35).

Much of the work about an ethic of caring has come from feminist scholars. By drawing our attention to another dimension of the work of caregiving, these scholars have brought the discussion into the open. In that light, Thompson (1998) asks us to maintain an awareness of the diversity and complexity of our world, urging us to initiate discussions that explore the differences in our relationships. She also adds that we cannot use any one social group as a model for care, as we are in danger of doing presently, by valorizing middle-class white women.

Philosopher Philip Hallie, spent many years examining the phenomenon of helping, exploring the behaviors and motivations of people ranging from rescuers of Jews during the Holocaust (1979) to volunteer maritime lifesavers in nineteenth century Boston Harbor (1997). There is a connection between his work regarding people who have chosen to help strangers, even at risk to themselves, and the exploration of the nature of caring. He calls it the "yes ethic"—the immediate, caring response to the needs of another human being. He is particularly interested in such a response to an unfamiliar person, for "strangers are different from beloved intimates. Helping is the nerve of intimacy, it is what intimacy is" (1997, p. 5). When people engage in the professions of nursing, teaching, or caregiving, they are usually in contact with strangers, who may become familiar. In contact with strangers, we must recognize differences on both practical and emotional levels.

Our connectedness and caring for each other contrasts with the dominant ideal of the independent individual. As parents, we are urged to encourage children to become independent, and as teachers we encourage students to be independent thinkers; the deeper emotional connections that we have can seemingly be ignored. Yet children and adults alike need a secure base, a base of connectedness and caring, from which to operate. The knowledge a toddler has of an available mother allows the toddler to venture, with increasing independence, carefully, further afield.

As we grow older we continue to need a sense of connection; it is vital to acknowledge the dependence we have on each other. Too often we take our connections, our unacknowledged secure base, for granted.

To not acknowledge our interdependence keeps the work of many caregivers unseen or unarticulated. Madeleine Grumet (1988) calls for us to make public the realm that has been considered private (i.e., the work of family, children, and caring). As we articulate and acknowledge this private realm and notice its systems of values and behaviors, we can begin to give it credit and make it visible. She writes, "And because so many teachers are women working in the shadows cast by the institutions of the public world and the disciplines of knowledge, I read their narratives to draw our life worlds out of obscurity so we may bring our experiences to the patriarchal descriptions that constitute our sense of what it means to know, to nurture, to think, to succeed" (p. 61). Lally (1995) states that the work of "infant/toddler care as a whole is not seen" (p. 59). The real work of caregivers is obscured by the public perception "that anyone can do it" (p. 59).

Historically the importance of women's work in general has been neglected. Ulrich (1990) points out that public records, such as bank records or newspapers or reports of merchants, clearly show the contributions of men to the economics and politics in late eighteenth-century America. The amount of flax seed sold and acres planted were recorded, but not the weeds the women pulled and the "combing, spinning, reeling, boiling, spooling, warping, quilling, weaving, bucking, and bleaching that transformed the ripe plant into finished cloth" (p. 29). In present times, the work of caring and tending and connecting continues to be extensively unnoticed and unacknowledged.

A Process, Not a Product

An *ethic of care*, an ethic of yes, does not fit neatly into the postindustrial notion of work as a product. It cannot be distilled into a series of tasks with an ultimate ideal performance. It cannot be quantified at 80 or 90 percent accomplished. While caring demands complex skills and energies of practitioners, it cannot be a product regulated by rules for behavior and output. In an attempt to assure quality, regulations are created to control behavior. But, unlike quality control in the factory line, establishing a relationship with an infant and her parents is not a matter of a set of behaviors. The complexity of the work of relationship cannot be rendered to a simplified form (Cannella and Kincheloe, 2002).

Within the field, most early childhood educators have moved beyond the behaviorism of the seventies when children were rewarded externally for the desired behavior. We are past offering Cheerios in a cup and stars on a chart. As caregivers and educators, we are paying attention to children's social and emotional growth (Corso, 2003), encouraging children's understanding and articulation of their emotions.

Caregivers are affected emotionally by their work with babies and families; they are also involved in a process of emotional growth. Understanding these emotions and the role they play in an individual caregiver's practice may help in acknowledging and articulating the complexity of the deeply relational and caring work in which early childhood educators are engaged. By describing the process, caregivers can begin to give voice to their experiences and the discussion can become public.

Making the Invisible Visible, or, Naming Pharaoh's Daughter

Focusing on the work of caring for and tending to others allows us to begin to put the inarticulate into words and illuminates aspects of the work not seen. To illustrate how ingrained and pervasive is the invisibility of the work of caregiving, I will share the following story:

> I worked hard to finish my proposal for my doctoral studies in time to join my father and sister in a family trip. I managed it and arrived tired and relieved. During our first evening together over a long and leisurely dinner I explained what I was working on. Over the years, my family had often heard from me about the finer points of child care and working with babies. I was speaking about the feminists' work on caring—all those small daily tasks which make life bearable.
>
> With the enthusiasm of the new scholar in the presence of a loving audience, I held forth on this topic probably longer than anyone other than close family would want to listen. After I had paused to breathe and to listen to their responses, my

father, the son of a Presbyterian minister, said, "It is the story of Mary and Martha."

My sister, who had probably not gone to Sunday School as often as I had, said, "Who?"

A few facts fell into place in my mind. "Mary and Martha!" I remembered, "Mary Magdalene sat at Christ's feet, hanging on his every word. Martha was in the kitchen making peanut butter sandwiches for the crowds, who arrived to listen to Jesus. Martha came to the kitchen door to tell Mary that she needed her help making the sandwiches for the multitudes. Christ said that Mary was doing her part by hanging on his every word."

I agreed. "You're right, Dad. It is time to celebrate Martha. Without her sandwiches, how many people would have come?"

This conversation rang bells. There were other unnamed women in the Bible. What about Pharaoh's daughter? I decided that I needed to pursue that angle.

Home from the trip, I looked up Pharaoh and his daughter in the Bible. In my edition, there was no name for her—the woman who was the first foster parent going nameless into the ages. And take note of her foster child, Moses!

I decided to ask my son David, who was home from Brandeis University and had taken a Jewish Studies course. "What was Pharaoh's daughter's name? The one who saved Moses."

He rattled off a name in Hebrew, Batya. Darn, I thought to myself; there goes my small theory. "What does the name mean?" I asked.

"What do you mean?"

"You know, Hebrew names often have a meaning, like Isaac means laughter, so I'm curious."

"Oh," he said, "it means Pharaoh's daughter."[1]

Articulating the ethos of caring helps draw attention to the work of caregivers. As Madeleine Grumet (1988) says, "the very act of description is a naming that splits the fusion of intimacy into words for the stranger" (p. 64). Imagine actually understanding the perspective of Martha, or of the Pharaoh's daughter. If we truly could comprehend the complex work of raising a child who had been set adrift, or understood the warmth and welcome behind Martha's providing food for hungry crowds, there would perhaps be an appreciation of the thought, intention, care, and energy required. Listening to the stories of caregivers should enrich our understanding of their work.

Chapter 5

Practitioner to Researcher: Telling Stories

I had several hospitalization experiences as a child. In the late 1940s and early 1950s when children went into a hospital, parents were discouraged from visiting. It was felt that the nurses could handle things better as children would get too upset by parental visits. No one looked closely at children's reactions to those separations from home and family.

By the early 1950s in London, John Bowlby had begun his work on attachment with the help of Dale Robertson, who filmed the effects of separation on very young children who were hospitalized. Bowlby saw that children, especially very young children, were depressed and over time became apathetic after being separated from their parents. By the mid-1950s, Robertson's films of hospitalized children and Bowlby's work on attachment theory were beginning to have an impact on the way children were treated in a hospital and elsewhere. It changed the way that people thought of children and their emotional capabilities.

In 1950 my initial experience in hospital was as a two-year-old. That time, separated from my parents, I had been in an oxygen tent fighting for breath while my parents had watched helplessly from another room. Hospital staff warned them not to go in. Staff reasoned that in my struggle to get to my parents I might use up all my energy.

Bowlby's work began to influence hospital procedures with children though adopting different practices took time and was uneven. My next experience was in a hospital that had not modified its procedures. In 1956 when I was eight years old and while in England, I had to have my adenoids removed. My father took me to the hospital, and I did not like either doctors or the smell of the hospital. We walked in and the smell, plus my terror, caused me to throw up all the way down the corridor. Once I was at the admitting desk the nurses took over and my father had to leave. Since parents were not allowed to visit any time during a child's hospitalization, I felt abandoned.

Life on the ward was clear. You did not make trouble for the nursing Sisters since they ruled with a firm, if not an iron, hand. I had to wait a day for the surgery since I had to get on a course of penicillin, which meant a shot morning and night. It hurt! But the code was you were not supposed to cry when you got it, because good boys and girls didn't. When I finally was home again, I could count five red dots on one side of my bottom and four on the other side.

I went for the surgery lined up with the other children. They took us in order and got us to count backward until the anesthetic took effect. I woke up in the middle of the night. Here again I knew the rule; stay in bed until morning and do not bother the nurses. But I was so thirsty I couldn't bear it. Finally gathering up all my courage I crept out of bed in the totally dark room and headed for the sink. I found water and, with a sigh of relief, went back to bed to sleep until morning.

I was kept there another three days under observation and on antibiotics. I was getting used to things, but I was mad at my mom and dad. How could they have left me there and not visited me? When they came to pick me up, eager to see me again, I ignored them; I wouldn't look at them.

A year later back in California, our doctor said I had to have my tonsils out. My mother, who understood me better than I thought she did and was a wise woman, asked to be referred to a doctor who did hypnosis with his patients if they asked for it. We went, and she asked if he would hypnotize me so that I would not worry myself into a frenzy. I have no memory of being hypnotized and apparently had slept well the week before I went to the hospital.

Even as I was preparing to have my tonsils out, I had memories of the year before, remembering throwing up when I walked into the hospital. In fact, I believed that this is what I did in hospitals: I threw up! So off I went to the hospital in California. The pediatric staff at this hospital must have been reading the work done by Bowlby and Robertson. The doctor who had hypnotized me must have been current in their work as well, because he had allayed my fears to the point that when I walked into the hospital I did not throw up. In fact, Dad asked if I wanted a milkshake and I said yes, and drank one!

When I went upstairs to the children's ward, my mother stayed with me until it was time to go to sleep. She was back in the morning to walk me to the operating room and was there when I woke up from the anesthetic. Apparently, the doctor had told me this is what would happen. I stayed only another night and then went home. I never felt abandoned and I have never been terrified of hospitals again.

The change in care that I experienced in the two settings probably reflected the impact of Bowlby's (1973; 1978) and his colleagues' research and thinking on attachment. James Robertson, who had worked with Anna Freud in her wartime nursery, went to work for Bowlby in 1948. He had observed the despair young children struggled with when left by their parents and in 1951, filmed a two-and-a-half-year-old girl undergoing an eight-day separation from her parents while in the hospital. The film illustrated some of Bowlby's ideas on attachment, showing the child's despair and bewilderment at being left by her parents; it shocked the pediatric world. Up to this point, doctors, nurses, and hospital policy had ignored or discounted children's fear and despair. Hospitals feared that parents would disrupt their procedures and Robertson and Bowlby's observations met with stiff resistance (Karen, 1994). By illuminating the experience of children separated from their parents in a strange and frightening situation, a new awareness developed. Fifty years later children's parents are often with their children right up until the operating room and can remain with them overnight during their hospital stay.

Understanding children's perspectives led to changes. Listening to the narratives of caregivers could provide direction for supporting good practice. As I embarked on the journey of researching the experience of caring for young children, I began to listen carefully to the stories around me. Whenever I was in a group of caregivers, supervisors of caregivers, or men and women who worked in other capacities with children and families, I told the story of Hector and his mother and tried to describe the variety of emotions that I had experienced in this work. People listened and responded with their own stories. People involved in caring for children understood the story and were able to share experiences of similar conflicted emotional situations; there appeared to be a need to speak and have their own stories heard.

At the beginning of the research journey, I thought I would focus on the emotional tensions inherent in caregiving. I remembered back to my early days of being with toddlers and thought of Hector as he hung on to the table leg, and I remembered the range of emotions I felt. I sensed his determination and felt his anger at his mother; I also felt his mother's growing impatience and anger at this public defiance. I felt caught, overwhelmed, and sad. I wanted to support Hector, to calm down his mother, and to get out of there, all at the same time. A variety of emotions had demanded my attention. Through my experiences, I was aware of other unnamed layers, and as I talked with caregivers, I felt the need to articulate an everyday narrative of caregiving.

How to Begin Articulating the Story

Robertson's work filming children in hospital settings drew our attention to the powerful feelings of children. Those feelings had gone unnoticed, unremarked until his documentary. Children have powerful feelings and they can activate powerful feelings in others. Caring for children, physically and emotionally, is work filled with complexity, multiplicity, and optimism. As Huebner (1999) has said, "Love and care provide not certainty, but hope" (p. 350). *Care* and *love* are terms often used casually; yet their meanings can vary given the speaker and the context. Love, care, and hope are qualities that cannot be easily measured; they speak of dimensions neither quantifiable nor verifiable. Benner and Gordon (1996) wrote, "The words 'caring' and 'to care' are some of the most heavily freighted in the English language. Like magnets, they attract the most noble images and conceits. Like veils, they conceal the most complex confusions and elisions" (p. 41).

Caregivers do not often get an opportunity to tell their stories of love and care, of struggles and tensions, except to each other. The voice of the caregiver has been absent from research literature until recently (Hatch, 1995; Leavit, 1994; Wien, 1995). In the last few years, there has been some call for the practitioners to

enter the dialogue (Doherty, et al., 2000; Goffin and Day, 1994).
Having worked with caregivers over time, I had heard some of the
stories and insights that could give texture and depth to the discussion of caring for babies. As a practitioner struggling with how to
best prepare future practitioners, and as a researcher, I wondered
what caregivers could tell me about their work and their solutions
to the complex issues involved. I imagined using their stories to
augment, challenge, and counterpoint my own, in looking more
deeply at this phenomenon of caring.

Using Stories

Often, in different settings, I have sat with others at round, child-
size tables and gone over the day by telling little stories of the
day's happenings and connecting those stories to stories from
other experiences, all the while trying to make meaning or sense
of a particular child, parent, or situation. As a supervisor or
teacher, I have used stories to illustrate a point, to help approach a
situation creatively, or to illustrate another perspective. As Cuffaro
(1995) has written, "early childhood teachers are storytellers. Each
day we have at least two or three stories to share" (p. 14). Through
stories, "experience and time work their way in inquiry" (Connelly
and Clandinin, 1990, p. 12).

Discussing the value of conversation and sharing ideas in gaining understanding and knowledge, Young-Bruehl and Bethelard
(2000, p. 18) quote a traditional Chinese story from the *I Ching:*
"A lake evaporates upward and thus gradually dries up; but when
two lakes are joined, they do not dry up so readily, for one replen-
ishes the other. It is the same in the field of knowledge.
Knowledge should be a refreshing and vitalizing force. It becomes
so only through stimulating intercourse with congenial friends
with whom one holds discussion and practices application of the
truths of life. In this way, learning becomes many-sided and takes
on a cheerful lightness, whereas there is always something ponder-
ous and one-sided about the learning of the self-taught."

Because telling stories is a natural and daily activity of ECEC
educators, it has been a natural way of beginning the discussion of
caring for infants. Smith (1987, pp. 34–35) says: "we have difficulty

asserting authority for ourselves. We have difficulty grasping authority for women's voices and for what we have to say. We are thus deprived of the essential basis for developing among ourselves the forms of thought and images that express the situations we share and make it possible to begin to work together." Telling stories and relating personal experiences is one way to begin to understand how the caregivers conceptualize and navigate their experiences and what meanings they bring to and take from their experiences; it is a way to begin to "work together."

Belenky, Bond, and Weinstock (1997) worked with rural, impoverished women, helping them to find their voices and to speak up for themselves and their children in a project called Listening Partners. They say, "gifted storytelling and gifted listening are the two capacities most needed for creating an ongoing dialogue that gives rise to powerful personal and collective statements that people who are just coming into voice can give to the world" (p. 298).

Caregivers have not often told their stories in the wider public arena. Tobin (1997, p. 13) reflects this in his statement, "The lives of young children and their caretakers are made up of a series of moments that are missing not necessarily because they are disturbing but because they are too quiet for us to hear, too small for us to see, so apparently uneventful that they fall beneath our threshold of attention." Using the caregivers' voices and stories stays close to their experiences. Polkinghorne (1988, p. 183) argues that narrative is one of "the most important forms for creating meaning."

Asking the Caregivers

The caregiver is key to the quality of the experience for the baby; the baby benefits from a caring person. As Howes and Hamilton (1993) state, "Child care in whatever form is basically a system of relationships with others" (p. 327). Leavitt (1994; 1995) has made us painfully aware of the impact of uninvolved caregiving where meaningful relationship is missing. The infant-toddler caregivers she observed seemed at best indifferent to children. Missing from her account is the caregivers' perspectives on their perceptions of the work caring for babies. In her 1994 article she cites her own unpublished research proposal, *Conversations with Caregivers: An Inquiry into the Work of Caregiving*. Beyond Leavitt's intention to speak with caregivers, there is little other research into the work of caring for babies from the perspective of the infant-toddler caregiver. Leavitt (1994, p. 97) herself notes that "sorely missing from the literature are investigations of caregivers' perspectives on their own caring experiences, and the particular problematics they face in these 'unnatural' contexts."

Few researchers have specifically spoken with infant-toddler caregivers for an in-depth look at their practice. Ayers (1991) says that "the secret of teaching after all is in the detail of everyday practice, the very stuff that is washed away in attempts to generalize about teaching" (p. 48). He looked at six preschool teachers and collected their stories of "the dailiness and the ordinariness of their lives with children" (p. 46). One of these teachers was a preschool teacher who returned to work with children after the birth of her daughter and chose to work in infant care.

There has been some investigation of mothers providing care in their home and how they perceive their jobs. For example, Nelson (1990) reports that "family daycare providers become enormously attached to the children in their care and, in some respects, giving them good care means treating them like their own. Yet these feelings cannot be allowed to flourish because they lack the privileges of motherhood and because they must commodify caregiving. Their emotional labor involves dismantling, or reducing the intensity of these same feelings" (p. 588).

Hopkins (1990), studied the "nursery nurses" in a day nursery in London to inquire "why the care of infants in day nurseries often becomes impersonal rather than intimate" (p. 99). She had group discussions with the caregivers and found they avoided intimate relationships with the children because they believed it would make their jobs easier. Their training had emphasized the importance of the children's independence and they had gone through routine activities such as feeding and changing of diapers in an impersonal manner, thinking it important to keep their own feelings at bay. With ongoing discussions and information about children's development, the caregivers began to develop deeper relationships with the babies. The result was that they were happier in their job and responded more positively to the infants' feelings. The children showed increases in language development and concentrated better on their play. "However," Hopkins states "the nurses' increased affection for the infants also made them more distressed about the inadequacy of the parenting which some of the infants received" (p. 106). Thus we see one of the tensions of a job that includes both rewards and dangers when involved in it deeply.

A preliminary exploration of such tensions is offered in a video produced with Alicia Lieberman (Lally and Gilford, 1996), where Lieberman, a researcher at the University of California at San Francisco Medical School, talked with caregivers and parents about their feelings around the care of their babies and explored possible solutions to dealing with their challenging emotional dynamics. On the video, caregivers exhibited intense emotions demonstrating some of the tensions that they experienced in their work. Parents are also shown exhibiting the intense emotions they experienced about their children. Lieberman demonstrated that caregivers must deal with both their own intense emotions and the intense emotions of both the parents and the babies.

The *You Bet I Care!* study done Canada-wide looked at wages, working conditions, and practices in child care centers (Doherty et al., 2000). In this study, researchers found that caregivers valued the relationships they had with children and felt they made a difference in children's lives; staff also reported that they did not feel valued or respected by the general public. This may well be due to the lack of understanding of the unseen, complex nature of the job. This lack of recognition may be a factor in the increase from the 1992 Canadian Child Care Federation's *Caring for a Living* study of staff who said they would not choose child care again as a career; the highest percentage was among the staff with the higher levels of education. A 2005 study on staff recruitment and retention found that staff's "commitment to the job is constantly eroded by their recognition that society considers child care a low status, low skilled position" (Doherty and Forer, 2005)

Another of the findings of the *You Bet I Care!* study was that staff "engage in considerable amounts of multi-tasking, that is, caring for children while also interacting with parents, or supervising students, or doing a task such as activity preparation" (Doherty et al., 2000, p. xv). The skills needed for this multitasking also go unrecognized and unacknowledged. Doherty et al., (2000) suggested "the perception of not being valued or respected contributes to poor staff morale and turnover, and may impede recruitment of new workers into the field" (p. 179). They recommended that the value of the people who work in the child care field be recognized, just as the importance of supporting the child's early years is being recognized.

Listening to caregivers discuss their practice offers insights into which educational resources were valuable for them and what supported them in a job that has both intellectual and emotional demands. "Thus, 'giving air time' to teachers is more than a sentimental or symbolic activity. It offers potential to change the nature of our conversation about important issues" (Schultz, 1994, p. 67). Changing the "nature of our conversation" requires listening to, attending to, and engaging with the stories.

Telling the Story to Others

Sharing narratives with others and gathering stories resulted in material full of individual perspectives and insights. Walsh, Tobin, and Graue (1993) suggest that qualitative research will not only elucidate the actual experiences *of* practitioners, but also highlight issues in an accessible manner *for* other practitioners. I wanted not only to approach caregivers in a way that would best elicit their stories, I wanted to share their stories with other practitioners. By sharing those stories I hoped that more stories would be told and narrative dialogue would begin.

In the past twenty years, research using a qualitative approach has emerged in ECEC. I have found this to be inspiring, as well as informative. Books like *The Erosion of Childhood* (Suransky, 1983), Lubeck's (1985) work observing in two different preschool programs, Jones and Reynolds's (1992) look at play through the vignettes of their own and teachers' observations, and Paley's (1979, 1986, 1990) stories and reflections have all inspired and informed me. Wien (1996) looked deeply at different teachers' classrooms and their reflections on how they organize and structure the day. Tobin, Wu, and Davidson's (1989) work was also helpful, as they used interviews and the voices of teachers, administrators, children, and parents to explore what preschools in three different cultures "are meant to do and to be" (p. 4).

The richness of this research and the interest in my own initial, informal questions inspired me to look deeply at caregivers' perspectives. The aforementioned works were based on listening and observing closely. Listening carefully, observing closely, and reflecting deeply seemed to be respectful stances to take toward the world of caregiving, and echoed those stances used in caregiving. Ayers (1991) comments in his work on the teaching lives of six early childhood practitioners, "the talk was everyday teacher talk, and so it was also value-talk and feeling-talk. It was talk of the ordinary and the mundane, yet it was talk that was frequently eloquent, consistently thoughtful, and always infused with a sense of care and connection" (p. 47). In my work, I hoped for a congruency of method and topic; I wanted to extend into research the skills that I already practiced as an early childhood educator.

Working with children and ECEC students over the years, I have deepened my learning through listening, observing, and wondering. These are useful skills in caregiving and I used them also to reflect on my practice, "using the same sensibilities and sensitivities that make for good teachers, friends, lovers, parents, and people— listening, conversing, interpreting, reflecting, describing and narrating" (Walsh, Tobin, and Graue, 1993, p. 465).

Working Narratively

Casper (1996, p. 14) says, "to be effective in working with very young children and their families, we need to understand their worlds. How do we usually go about learning what is really important to others? We observe and listen. We reflect." This is also true of strong research. As sharing stories is a comfortable, familiar mode of discussing work for caregivers, using a narrative approach is a natural and appropriate mode of research. Polkinghorne (1988) writes that discerning "narrative meaning is a cognitive process that organizes human experiences into temporally meaningful episodes" (p. 1). To understand the caregiving experience, I needed to listen to caregivers' stories.

Several years ago, I attended a conference where the keynote speaker said that, in his culture, it was bad manners to tell another's story; you have a right only to your own story. He went on to say that only when *all the stories are told, then we will have the whole story.* I appreciated his concept; it leaves no one out and suggests an endless array of stories. I hope that it will not be too unmannerly to allow the stories of others to be interwoven with my own story. The comedian Sandra Shamas (1997) said in an interview on CBC, "I tell my story so that you can remember yours." Using narrative opens up possibilities on many levels.

As stated earlier, the voices and stories of caregivers have not been heard and we do not see them in the research literature. As Hauser and Jipson (1998, p. 4) wrote, "Intuitively, the idea of storytelling seemed to provide an appropriate way to relate our explorations of the many differences we identified among the experiences of the women with whom we worked and studied. By telling stories, we could locate the diverse historical, cultural, and socioeconomic positions women have held as they have been excluded and then integrated into the public sphere of formal early childhood education, all the while continuing to be primarily relegated to the quasi-domestic work of caring for and socializing young children." Stories and narratives capture the complexity of the daily work of caregivers. I also felt it was important to, as Barone (1990) suggests, "lift the veils of objectivity to see the face of an author making choices about method, language, plot" (p. 320). As a result, I have woven my own stories as a caregiver and early childhood educator into this work.

Researcher as Insider

As a researcher, I was also an ECEC practitioner with a wealth of my own stories; I was an insider. My knowledge and experience of caregiving is part of this research. Some of the women I interviewed were my friends. For years, I had been talking with some of these caregivers, and we had a common language of anecdote and narrative to explain our work and our approaches.

Working as a practitioner in Turkey, New York City, Berkeley, Vancouver, and Victoria, and with a variety of children and families, I have become aware of the many realities and the many layers of perceptions of the world. Working in both rural and urban settings, working with young parents and with some parents whose language I did not speak, working with children who could read at two and with others who only first spoke at two and a half, I had struggled with "the complexity of the everyday life of the early childhood institution" (Dahlberg, Moss, and Pence, 1999, p. 95). Cannella (1997, p. 170) suggests, "multiple human realities will require that we become comfortable with uncertainty, that we accept ambiguity." Through this research, I began to articulate and acknowledge some of the uncertainties.

As an insider, I brought an understanding of the work that was intellectual, emotional, and visceral. Over years of working with children, teaching ECEC students, and reflecting on related issues, I have developed a philosophical base grounded in my own learning and experience, what Polanyi (1958) calls "personal knowledge" He notes, "our intelligence falls short of the ideal of precise formalization" (p. 53). *Personal knowledge* includes skills, which are both articulated and unspecifiable, and connoisseurship that is the ability to appraise the situation. As well, I agree with Clifford's (1986) position, that "insiders studying their own cultures offer new angles of vision and depths of understanding. Their accounts are empowered and restricted in unique ways" (p. 9). I used my own stories to make sense of, and to resonate with, my participants' stories. We exchanged stories as we gained understanding from each other. Stories clarified statements and signified that the other's point of view had been heard.

Using an idea from Behar (1996), Jayapal (2000) reminds us that "even the best objectivity is filled with subjectivity, that perhaps marking ourselves as 'vulnerable observers' is the only justice we can do to those people and places we write about, to our readers and to ourselves" (p. 7). By leaving behind the position of the "detached observer," I tried to remain open and vulnerable as I wrote about relationships and working within relationship. As Meloy (1994) stated, "The complexity of the researcher as the human instrument has only begun to be explicated" (p. xiii). Just as the work of caring for babies involves many dimensions, so does the type of inquiry I embarked on. Munro (1998, p. 11) reminds us that "all stories are partial, the teller always 'in flux'." I wove my own story among the narratives of my participants to, as Munro says, "acknowledge the intersubjective nature of knowledge" (p. 6). These stories speak to each other, and as a collection they strengthen each other, both echoing themes and presenting new perspectives while deepening the discussion of the issues. As Hauser and Jipson (1998) write, "whenever two people share a story a new one emerges" (p. 5). Connelly and Clandinin (1990) state, "We also need to tell our own stories as we live our own collaborative researcher/teacher lives. Our own work then becomes one of learning to tell and live a new mutually constructed account of inquiry in teaching and learning" (p. 12).

We all have stories to explain ourselves. We have stories we try to live up to. We have meanings that guide our practice. Lagerway (1998, p. 38) writes that "we hang the events of our lives upon narrative structures and turn them into stories. We select and arrange fragments into orderly sequences, telling our stories as if they had inherent beginnings, middles, and endings, as if cause and effect has been operative and visible. Thus our stories, and the ones we hear and read, achieve an authority as they resonate with our own desires for understanding and significance."

As I moved from the role of practitioner to that of researcher, I was aware of how influential my practitioner's viewpoint was on the research. Telling my own story seemed one way to pull my perspective into the research, as well as helping to fill out the picture of baby care. Through this process, I hoped to keep alive the tension that is inherent in research. I wanted the voices of the caregivers to speak and yet I, ultimately as a researcher, shaped the process. The stories and the conversations have helped me reflect on my own experiences, allowing me to think more deeply about issues that I had already struggled with and that needed further perspectives. Caregivers highlighted issues for me that I had previously ignored or neglected.

Vivian Paley (1997, 1995, 1992, 1990, 1986, 1979) uses stories of her teaching to explore larger questions that emerge from her young students. One year, she explored the uses of superheroes in her class. Another year, she wondered about a boy "who would be helicopter." Using her own experiences to explore her understanding of how to relate to the children in her class, the answers she came up with are not necessarily solutions for another's teaching, but the process of her reflection on her own knowledge, her own experiences, and her own values, was important for me. It is this recognition of ourselves as part of the story that is important. As I worked with caregivers' narratives, my own narrative became an essential part of the story.

Tobin and Davidson (1990) assert that "teachers participating in research are vulnerable" (p. 273). If I share my stories, I hope in some measure to share some of my participants' vulnerabilities. My awareness of their vulnerability and the knowledge that I could anticipate at what point a caregiver might feel uncomfortably exposed are tensions I realized I must hold.

I listened to their stories "for resonance between the inner and the outer, an echo that brings the attention into focus" (Bateson, 1984, p. 163). I tried to understand what in their stories connected to my stories, and what these stories told me about the process of caring for babies. I was closely attentive to their stories, and my own, to find what I was learning about the processes of caring within a multitude of relationships—infant-toddler caregiver, researcher, early childhood instructor, doctoral student.

Working in Relationship: The Interviews/Conversations/Stories

I explored these questions from within a relationship with this group of women where, against a background of trust and empathy, I hoped the caregivers' stories would emerge. I was seen as a colleague by the study's participants, known by them as someone involved in the field; I knew we could have conversations leading to an exchange of narratives. Being a researcher was a new role for me. My list of research questions helped me stay focused and gave a weight to the conversations I had with the participants.

As we listened to each other, our interview/conversation found its own natural flow. Within each conversation, I was attentive to the opportunities for enlightenment. Together we would generate meaning and insight. My questions would merely begin the conversation and together we would explore the experience of caring for babies, creating insights, and understanding together.

The discussions were animated at times; voices rose and words spilled over each other. Since they had volunteered to participate in these discussions, I assumed that caregivers wanted to talk with me. Even the two women who had not met me before were ready to discuss their jobs at length. Through the stories and discussions with the caregivers, I found an insight that "refers to that depth of under-standing that comes by setting experiences, yours and mine, familiar and exotic, new and old, side by side, learning by letting them speak to one another" (Bateson, 1994, p. 14). We recognized each other's stories and feelings, even though they were often different.

In our conversations, there were places where we found reflected stories; there were common threads that wove in and out of the talk, and there were places where we surprised each other and offered the other a new perspective. Someone would tell a story that reminded me of a story, which might be a story we knew in common or reminded me of a story that I shared with them. By sharing such a story, there was an opportunity to see if I had understood the caregiver or if it triggered other thoughts about the matters we were discussing. Within the narratives were common threads that I shared with the caregivers, for example a caregiver's sadness when a baby she felt close to left her program and the experience of finding relationships with parents difficult at times. There were similarities and differences in the ways people coped with each issue.

Trying to be responsive, I followed the flow of the talk. I asked questions at points to clarify the narrative, or to try and understand a caregiver's experience more fully. Just as I try to understand chil-dren and ECEC students, I wanted to understand the experiences of these women. Which issues did they all find difficult? How did they cope with, and negotiate the meaning of, these issues?

There was also an improvisational quality to the interviews, which is always necessary when interacting with people as gen-uinely as possible. I could not predict the course of each conversa-tion and tried to have no preconceived ideas about the specific concerns of each participant. For example, one participant was concerned by the lack of training of her co-workers and the lack of cohesion among the staff. I spent more time on this issue with her, and she gave me an understanding of the importance of co-work-ers that the women who had highly functional situations did not.

Multiplicity of Views

Within relationship, each of us has the possibility of discovering other ways of seeing and experiencing the world. Because we care for or are interested in that person, we take the time to see what is important to her, we struggle to understand her choices, we try to hear what she is saying, and sometimes we succeed. Working with a variety of families in different settings has taught me that there are many levels of meaning and many differing realities, and my own understanding of a situation is usually enhanced when I consult with others with whom I am working. I was also aware of the variety of roles that one brings to a relationship and how those roles might influence that relationship. When I interviewed the women who knew me, we were friends and colleagues. For several of the caregivers I had been a teacher, which again shifts the relational dynamics. Each role has subtly different sets of rules.

Beyond the immediate relationships I had in terms of the interviews and research, my other relationships hover in the background. I was not only an early childhood educator, but a mother, stepmother, daughter, sister, wife, activist in my local community. Each of these roles impacted my thinking and my conversations. Women who knew me well asked about my children or shared information about their children, who were now mothers themselves. These stories were not an explicit part of the material to be analyzed, and yet they were in the background, influencing the conversations and the understandings that we brought forth.

Multiple roles cannot be untwined. Caregiving involves energy from physical, intellectual, spiritual, and emotional levels. It demands one's whole being, with each facet contributing to the process. While inquiring about the nature of this practice, I worked to bring my whole being to the task.

Ethics of Being a "Vulnerable Observer"

The tensions and difficulties caregivers experience in their work are seldom discussed publicly, and how they resolve or live with those tensions is not often articulated. Working with babies involves not only the mind, but also the heart; issues of the heart are often private matters. Working with babies also means communicating on a predominantly nonverbal level, where we are forced to pay attention with all of our senses and to communicate in many different ways. Being in the presence of a baby creates hormonal changes in the body that influence thinking and feeling. Parker Palmer (1983) writes "that knowing draws not only on our senses and our reason, but on our intuitions, our beliefs, our actions, our relationships, and on our bodies themselves" (p. xii). Being fully present is called for in this work, and how to speak of it is not clear.

Within the research relationship, I attended to being responsive to what the caregivers were telling me, remaining aware and present to each unique person and situation. Delpit (1995) suggests that this approach focuses on "learning to be part of the world rather than trying to dominate it—on learning to see rather than merely look, to feel rather than touch, to hear rather than listen: to learn, in short, about the world by being still and opening myself to experiencing it. If I realize that I am an organic part of all that is, and learn to adopt a receptive, connected stance, then I need not take an active, dominant role to understand; the universe will, in essence, include me in understanding" (p. 92).

Being responsive, I also intended to be responsible. While *responsive* means making an answer or reply, the *Oxford Dictionary* (Fowler and Fowler, 1964) defines being *responsible* as answering to something or fulfilling a trust. Being responsive is one aspect of the dynamic of a caring relationship, yet one is also responsible for one's reactions. Responsiveness is alluded to by Bateson (1994) when she writes that "the gift of personhood is potentially present in every human interaction, every time we touch or speak or call one another by name, yet denial can be very subtle too, inflicted in the failure to listen, to empathize, to attend" (p. 62). Within my relationship with the caregiver-participants, I sought to be responsive. I have been discerning and responsible both for the use of information gathered in our interviews and in my treatment of the relationships themselves. Belenky and her associates (1997) state that "communication is tied to trust, and fostering another requires attending to the other" (p. 81). Being responsive and responsible are necessarily intertwined.

By being responsive and responsible to the babies in their care, caregivers develop a special relationship with a baby. Gerstenzang notes, "although babies will seek attention from almost everyone, they will light up for a few special people and you know when you are one of them. It is a gift that you accept from them—a gift with an obligation to love and protect them" (Gerstenzang, 2005, p. 55). I hoped to take this sensibility with me.

Vanier (1998) defines this trust as "the intuitive knowledge that we are safe in the hands of another and that we can be open and vulnerable, one to another" (p. 43). With the women I knew well, there existed a trust and understanding that Grumet (1988) says comes from "time and space and specificity" (p. 165). With these women, I could easily share stories of the joys and sorrows we had known working with babies and their families. A participant said after our first interview that she would not be able to tell me "these things" if she did not trust me.

Aware of the need for trust and the responsibility for not betraying that trust, I was concerned about establishing a sense of safety for all the participants. Donawa (1999) writes, "a trusting relationship requires ongoing judgment and observation; when we trust someone, we trust them to be attentive, observant, and discriminating in the expression of their trustworthiness toward us" (p. 25). My relationship with these women would have its own course, but as well as creating a safe external interview space, I needed to clear the way within myself to create a place of safety for them. I needed to be aware of not only the words spoken in the interviews and of my perceptions of our interactions, but I also needed to keep a heightened awareness of my inner reactions, believing that if those who volunteered to speak with me could sense my openness and my freedom from judgment, they would respond more freely.

Looking at the roots of the word *interview* the literal interpretation is "to see one another" (Fowler and Fowler, 1964). As I interviewed these women who looked after babies, I wanted to understand them within their contexts; I wanted the interview to be a dialogue that we shared. My goal was to maintain an open and nonjudgmental attitude because, as Josselson (1995) says, "If we listen well, we will unearth what we did not expect" (p. 30). We need listeners to whom we can tell stories.

By paying attention both to the small voice inside and to what was occurring contextually, I was most apt to be appropriately responsive and able to establish a space of trust. Trust is a complex concept; the demands of its implications—confidence, safety, security, hope—are difficult to fulfill. There is a tension inherent in trust, as it can easily and inexplicably be disrupted. While I write of trust and its importance, lurking behind trust is the danger of betrayal. Ancient roots of the word *troth* connect the word *trust* to truth. *Troth* is a linguistic root of both trust and truth; one of its meanings is "promise" (Fowler and Fowler, 1964). Perhaps the most we can attain is the promise of trust and truth. Promise suggests that both trust and truth rest on the goodwill of the person making the promise. Noddings (1984) suggests that this good will is *fidelity*: "fidelity is not seen as faithfulness to duty or principle but as a direct response to individuals with whom one is in relation" (p. 497). A promise of fidelity called on my responsibility to each individual woman and to our relationship.

The caregivers have trusted me with their stories, and I have trusted their stories to be meaningful representations of their beliefs about practice. They have trusted I would understand and explicate the meanings of what they said and also what was behind their words. I have worked to honor that trust.

Chapter 6

Responsive Caregiving

Observation 1, October 1999, 9:30 in the morning:

The center was very peaceful when I walked into the room. The noise level was low; the overhead lights were off, so the light was subdued and peaceful. I always wonder why more centers don't keep their lights low, as it is so effective in lowering the energy of a room.

I took off my shoes, and put on my slippers, a ritual marking that I am entering another space, a space intended for babies. I hung up my jacket and went to the sink to wash my hands. There was a faint odor of soiled diapers in the air and it reminded me that Isaac, my six-year-old son, had warned me to be careful to wash my hands "because babies can get smelly."

I walked into the room that opens into the toddler side and stood for a moment to watch the toddlers in action. They eyed me curiously and went about their business. I moved to the baby side and opened the half door that separates the babies from the young ones who are walking.

The baby area is not big: ten feet by ten feet. There is a space off to the side where one caregiver can feed a baby at a table or on her lap. The nap room is just off this room.

When I walked in Ra (eleven months) was eating, sitting at the little table with Jade sitting beside him. I said "hi" to Jade, and Ra swiveled to look at me. He was finger-feeding himself bananas,

71

toast, and pancakes cut into pieces. Quite a bit of food was going to his mouth, but how much he really ate was not clear.

I turned and said "hello" to Sheryl and sat on a pillow. Dina (two and a half months) was lying on the quilt, and Sal and Gage were investigating the stairs. Sal was crawling. I discovered she is eight months old and Gage is a year.

Ra was finished with breakfast and was put on the floor. He fussed a bit as he pulled himself forward with his hands. As he headed to me he ran into a small brightly colored truck and stopped to investigate. He continued to come closer to me. He saw a plastic bottle that was filled with sparkles and stopped to examine it. Meanwhile, Gage was standing at the window saying "AHHHHH" in a loud voice to the toddlers outside. (He used to be with the toddler group of children, but this year he is the oldest on the baby side. He misses his friends and his caregiver.) He did not seem unhappy, just intent on communicating with the group outside.

On his tummy Ra pulled up to eye my note-taking and was patting my journal. He turned to watch Gage at the window. Jade was holding Dina and the baby looked very cozy on her lap. Sal was trying to get to the window alongside Gage. She couldn't pull herself up to stand and look out as he was doing. She was in his vicinity, attracted by the energy he was focusing outside. She strained to stand up beside him.

Ra was at my knee trying to stand, and he was drooling.

Ra went to Jade fussing. Jade explained she would put Dina down and then would get his blanket for him. She put Dina down and went to get Ra's blanket and bottle. "Ra, here's your blanket. I have your bottle. You know what that means."

The Babies

Working with babies and toddlers is exhausting, exhilarating, and complex. A busy job, it requires both physical and mental stamina. A variety of rituals and routines structure the day, though surprises are frequent and guaranteed to disrupt any routine.

I spent approximately seven to ten hours observing in each center in order to get an understanding of the context in which each caregiver worked. These observations gave me an opportunity to remember my experiences with babies and toddlers and my experience in an infant-toddler center. At each center I glimpsed being a caregiver in that particular setting and tried to imagine working there.

In each center my observations differed, as they were dependent on what was occurring at the time, what was of most interest to me at the moment, and whether I was engaged in conversation with a caregiver or a baby who left me little time to make notes. While writing of women who work with babies, however, it is crucial to not forget the baby. Though each setting and therefore each observation is unique, I have picked examples that illustrate some aspects of the work. The previous observation and the one following are merely glimpses into the world of nurturing babies and toddlers.

Looking after three babies, feeding and caring for them, takes time and energy. A caregiver uses sensitive observational skills to learn a baby's signals of hunger or fatigue. Recognizing the cue indicating that a baby wants her bottle or her blanket takes careful attention to, knowledge of, and experience with that specific baby. In healthy situations outside of the home environment, baby and caregiver interact with an intimate trust and knowledge of the other where the baby can relax knowing that the caregiver will respond sensitively to her messages.

This knowledge of another is discovered over time. Knowing how closely to hold someone, recognizing a tone of voice, anticipating what someone's next move might be, is a process that evolves over time for both baby and caregiver. This type of knowledge of another person is expected or hoped for in personal relationships, but successful caring for infants and toddlers *demands* this type of knowledge from paid workers. Caregivers are asked to enter an intimate space, to actively seek a warm, close relationship with the babies for whom they care.

Toddlers require different rhythms and responsiveness from caregivers.

The Toddlers

Observation 3, October 1999, mid-morning:

All of these toddlers are approximately eighteen months. It is difficult to capture the activity that swirls around me. There is an ebb and flow of emotions, activities, and energies. It is challenging to observe, as my attention is like the toddlers themselves, moving and shifting as they do. Perhaps I am picking up on their energy. I like being here and I like their energy.

They are eyeing me with standoffish curiosity, but most are mainly interested in each other and their caregivers. As they eye me they glance at their caregivers.

Some cry as their caregiver leaves with another child.

They notice tiny details with joy and intensity, delighting in the discovery.

They are moving, running, climbing, pushing someone for the sheer joy of it.

The caregivers, calmly and quietly, are describing movement, texture, surface—"It's slippery, wet, rough."

The children watch each other with concern, curiosity, familiarity.

"Ah! Oh! Oh! EEEEE! Hi!" are their sounds—communicating with sound and conviction.

Now and then a child glances at me, approaches me carefully.

They taste the world, and the outside of the shed, and each other.

Their emotions are immediate, while caregivers respond quietly, "You, OK?"

"Austin needs to be changed." "You're upset when I go in." "Look at your hand, your finger!"

Touching, bumping, cuddling, pointing, colliding, the movement seems continuous.

Noses running, tears flowing, "Come sit on my lap," standing still, crying, desolate, Mel, a caregiver, puts out her arms. Elisha lifts hers and Mel picks her up.

Others run and smile and laugh, aware of Elisha's unhappiness and yet enjoying the sun, the warmth of late October.

This morning Elisha is feeling fretful. Mel tends to Elisha and gives her her attention.

But others are teasing, taking Elisha's soother and running, "Let's go get it," says Mel to Elisha.

Dawn, a caregiver, playing guitar, knees bending, bodies bouncing, everyone at the guitar, dancing with feet and bodies, someone is spinning in circles. Another rubs her hands on the bench, licks it, dreamily listening to the music.

Another one walks down the slide and hides her face in Dawn's skirt, "peekaboo."

Up the stairs, down the slide on your bottom, on your feet, sideways, casually, confidently.

Three lined up at the top of the slide, Al slides down, Cathy slides on her back, someone else tries to climb up, caregiver moves over to help children pay attention.

Elisha bursts into tears, today she seems to be overwhelmed by any difficulty. Cathy runs away with Elisha's soother, Mel asks if she is going to give it to Elisha, Cathy chants, "Lisha! Lisha!"—others continue to climb and slide. Elisha cries, Cathy approaches, Mel suggests Elisha ask Cathy. Mel says, "Let's ask Cathy." Elisha puts out her hand

and Cathy gives it back and Elisha dissolves in tears. Her crying is an unhappy thread in the morning motions.

To take observation notes while watching the toddlers, I had to work quickly; my attention darted from here to there. Writing quickly, I caught only part of the action.

The Centers

The British Columbia Child Care Licensing Regulations clearly state that for the group care of children under thirty months, for a group of nine to twelve children there must be one infant-toddler educator, one early childhood educator, and one assistant; a ratio of 1:4. There must be no more than twelve in one group. A separate sleeping room must be provided that is "not located in an activity area." The regulations outline the minimum space requirements for inside and outside and also cover health and safety regulations. All of the participating centers conformed to the regulations and were licensed.

Though all the programs were nonprofit and licensed, each one had its own unique character. Programs involving the care of children generally develop in response to the needs of the families they are serving. Each of these programs had emerged to serve a particular community and had a unique history.

From my observations and discussions, I learned that each place had its particular rituals and routines. Rituals and routines have unique and historical ways of growing. These are what Wein (1995) calls "scripts for action." These scripts, or routines, are what make the day more predictable. Scripts can free people up as they provide known solutions to problems and known formats for activities. Each center relied on scripts for action in different ways. Scripts can be set in place and not questioned or, evolving, they can be used as long as they are useful and questioned at intervals as to their continued usefulness.

Each center had been influenced by Magda Gerber's (1979) philosophy of primary caregiving, yet each had interpreted it in its own way. Three of the four centers were able to assign one caregiver to three babies for most of the day, while the fourth center had a looser interpretation of the concept. Each center served a different population, and the role of caregiver was modified by the needs of the parents. For example, the *school-based center* worked with young parents and the staff was very involved in the young mothers' lives. The *work-site infant center,* used primarily by professional families, needed staff who could not only articulate clearly the center's philosophy and expertise, but also could speak clearly to the issues raised by these parents.

The *school-based center* served twelve young mothers and their babies, developed in response to a need identified by an alternative school serving young women under the age of nineteen with very few resources as they took on the parenting role. Babies' ages ranged from a few weeks to three years old. The day ran from 8 a.m. to 4 p.m., with a half day on Friday. Staff—four caregivers and a supervisor—worked the same schedule, which allowed them to share the day from beginning to end with each other. The supervisor did the administrative work, supported and worked with staff, usually relieving people for lunch. As the mothers were going to school in the same building, there was frequent contact with them.

The focus of this program was on building relationships with both mothers and babies and through these relationships support was offered to both parent and child. A primary caregiver system was in place, with each caregiver assuming the care (feeding, diapering, and sleeping) for three babies and maintaining contact with three mothers and any other family members involved. Two caregivers worked in a team; their six babies became a group. This system offered flexibility to the caregivers so they were free to spend one-on-one time with a baby when necessary and to have another adult with whom to share the work. Caregivers sometimes stayed with their babies for two years, moving with them from the infant side of the room to the toddler side.

The caregivers in the school-based program were Jade, Dawn, Mel, and Sheryl. All of these women participated in my interviews. Jade had been there ten years, Dawn had been in the program seven years, Sheryl had been at the program for one year, and Mel had just begun. The staff met regularly once a week to discuss issues and concerns. They also met regularly with the school staff to discuss common concerns and strategies. Other informal meetings might occur as needed, such as at the beginning of the year when new families were starting.

The *institution-based center* was part of an agency that delivered several different programs and offered a wide range of child care options. The daycare center provided care for preschool-aged children. Other programs were available for children needing out-of-school care, and infant care became available when the Board became aware of the community's need. The daycare met the needs of working families and was open from 7:30 a.m. to 5:30 p.m. There was space for twelve children under eighteen months, though only eleven spots were filled when I observed. Usually three caregivers worked with the babies for a ratio of 1:4, with a qualified supervisor who sometimes helped out when a caregiver was away or sick. Of the three caregivers, one was an infant-toddler educator and the other two were early childhood educators without their infant-toddler specialty. Lynn, one of my participants, was the infant-toddler educator and had been with the program for a year and a half.

In this program, staff met once a month for one and a half hours after work. Caregivers worked an eight-and-a-half hour day with a half hour off for lunch. When children were eighteen months they moved to the toddler program. The caregiver remained with her program and did not move to programs with the children.

Primary caregiving was done a bit differently in this setting. Each caregiver had four families with which they communicated.[1] They had evolved a system where all the diapers of twelve babies were to be changed at set intervals in the day; this task was rotated among the caregivers. Mealtime was also a task that was rotated among the staff.

The *college-based infant center* was part of the child care services for staff and students. The program was established to meet the needs of students and staff who had a difficult time finding child care for their three-to-five-year-old children. The age limits were extended to include toddlers and infants when the demand grew. The center was open from 8 a.m. to 5 p.m., with staff working a seven-hour day including an hour's unpaid lunch break and two paid coffee breaks. The center closed for eight weeks in the summer. When I observed, they had six babies under eighteen months, with two caregivers, both of whom are infant-toddler educators, and a regular part-time person who came in at lunch. As this center was a component of a larger child care complex, a director did the administrative work. Rachel, who spoke with me, had been with the program for five years, either full-time or part-time.

In this setting each staff person cared for three babies and was very conscious of feeding and diapering the babies for whom she was responsible. The staff met once a month, at closing time for an hour, and although staff were not paid for this meeting time, they took an hour off in lieu of pay.

There was a separate program for toddlers and as this program had its own staff, the babies had to make a transition to new staff and surroundings. Their primary caregiver would take them to the new room for visits before the actual move in an effort to make the transition gradual.

The *work-site infant center* in the downtown core cared for twelve babies under eighteen months. The staff was comprised of four caregivers, and one of the caregivers was also the supervisor. There was a regular substitute to free the supervisor to do her administrative work. The staff were infant-toddler educators, and Mary, whom I interviewed, had been with the program for ten years. Several parents worked close by and could drop by at lunch or coffee break to visit their babies.

After the babies turned eighteen months old, the parents had to find a new program for their children. This center wanted to keep the children longer, but had found that its space can only accommodate the twelve babies. Staff was paid for a seven-hour day and worked a seven-hour and twenty-two minute day so that they could each have a day off each month. They had a regular substitute who came in to provide consistent care. The hours of the center were 8 a.m. to 5 p.m. The staff met every other week for two hours. They were paid for this meeting, as it was after work hours.

Although the variations in the centers' contexts were not initially my primary concern, during the interviews it became clear that the contexts themselves created conditions that affected the caregiver's experience and stories, and their caregiving. Personnel in each center structured and organized time differently. The institution-based program had the longest hours as the parents needed that time, while the school-based program operated the shortest number of hours as they followed the school day. In each center, there was time for meeting and debriefing as a staff. The school-based infant center, where the babies had left by 3:30 p.m., was unique in having ample time to debrief problems or issues as they arose. While each program did have some meeting time set aside for staff, commitments to meeting and discussion differed.

The Caregivers

The infant-toddler educators who participated in this study— Mary, Lynn, Rachel, Dawn, Jade, Mel, and Sheryl—were a varied group in terms of age, education, and experience, yet all were licensed infant-toddler educators and committed to the work that they did. As there were no male caregivers working with infants, I was unable to include a male perspective. This is consistent with the national statistics, which found that 98 percent of the teaching staff in day care centers are women (Doherty et al., 2000). It would have been valuable to include the voice of a male caregiver, but males who do work in the field almost always work with preschoolers or older children.

Gender aside, this group was not representative of infant-toddler caregivers in Canada. The national picture of caregivers as reported in the Canada-wide study on wages, working conditions, and practices in child care centers, *You Bet I Care!* (Doherty et al., 2000), indicates that 71 percent of all staff are holders of a one-, two-, or three-year ECEC certificate. An ECEC-related BA or higher degree was reported by 11 percent of the staff. Three of the seven (43 percent) in my study's group had an ECEC-related BA, and all seven (100 percent) had at least a two year certificate.

Each of the four most experienced caregivers has more than five years experience with babies, and has at least ten years experience in early childhood education overall. These women were articulate and thoughtful about their jobs. As I observed them in their settings, I found each had her own style of being present and responsive to the infants in her care. Each of their narratives represents a different style of reflection, perspective, and framing of practice.

I enjoyed talking with the caregivers; everyone was willing, even eager, to talk with me. As an insider and known to the caregivers, they knew that I understood and valued their work. Because the work of looking after infants and toddlers is often ignored or dismissed in the wider community, there are not many opportunities beyond the work setting to discuss the work of caring for babies. My own memories may also have limited me as I listened to their stories. The philosopher Michael Polanyi (1958) wrote, "For, as human beings, we must inevitably see the universe from a center lying within ourselves and speak about it in terms of a human language shaped by the exigencies of human discourse" (p. 3). However, I believe the trust and rapport created by my comprehension of the work outweighed the possible limitations of my listening as an insider.

Each woman was multifaceted and multidimensional in her practice. Each caregiver took a thoughtful approach to her work and highlighted the meanings she derived from its difficulties and rewards. For example, Lynn had difficulty with the women she worked with because they did not share her philosophy and this dissonance was one of the foci of my conversations with her as I had known similar situations and could go between my experience and hers. My experience gave me clues as to how she might be feeling and some of the issues with which she might be dealing. I had to be careful, however, to not impose my reactions on hers, but rather to use my experience to connect with her experience.

Caregivers who had less dissonant work environments had other concerns. I did ask everyone about teamwork and its function in their settings, but as a concept it had become background for those in settings where good teamwork was a given. I explored the physical, sensual nature of the work as this dimension emerged with Dawn more pervasively than with others who focused on some other aspect of the job. I understood her perspective as I had experienced the pleasure of holding an infant and watched the pleasure toddlers experienced as they moved and climbed. Each of my conversations flowed in the direction of a caregiver's interest or concern as I perceived it.

Relationship was a central issue for the caregivers. They all became animated and excited talking about the babies in their care, their genuine care was evident, and these relationships were multidirectional. Other relationships were part of this care for a baby. Studying more closely, I followed the threads of connected knowing and understanding that each caregiver considered and their definitions of the connections with their work, families, each other, and themselves.

Relationship

"A baby cannot exist alone, but is essentially part of a relationship," according to Winnicott (1987). Babies are "designed" to interact with their caregivers, to enlist their help to survive. There has been much focus on how a responsive relationship contributes to healthy infant development (e.g., Ainsworth and Bell, 1977; Ainsworth et al., 1978; Howes, Phillips, and Whitebrook, 1992; Howes and Smith, 1995). *From Neurons to Neighborhoods* (Shonkoff and Phillips, 2000), a recent study of the current developments in the field of early development, states that the "quality of care ultimately boils down to the quality of relationship between the child care provider or teacher and the child" (p. 314). A relationship assumes the engagement of at least two people, and to be successful both people must be involved and committed. This encourages what Pikler (1979) calls "a sound, reciprocal, close human relationship" (p. 100). The women I interviewed were both involved and committed.

A picture emerged of the layers of relationship involved in caregiving. The term *infant-toddler caregiver* suggests that this work is only about relationship with the baby. Yet babies have parents and other family members, and caregivers must also relate to these people. In addition, staff members working closely with each other during the day must ideally develop safe and supportive relationships among themselves. These interwoven layers of connections often have competing pulls, and the strong relationship to one's self offers a balancing perspective to other relationships. Caregivers spoke about the various facets of these relationships and the possible tensions within them.

Being self-aware, responding sensitively to the baby and parent, working harmoniously together with staff, all require skill and thoughtfulness, require trust in one's self and in one's co-workers. Responding consistently and appropriately to the baby builds the infant's trust in the caregiver. While one of the origins of the word *trust* is "faithfulness" (Fowler and Fowler, 1964), one could ask in whom to put one's faith. The caregiver is in a critical position and must be reliable, attuned, and responsive to children, parents, and her work place. She must be able to rely on both her co-workers and herself. This practice calls for more than just a set of behaviors; it calls for total engagement of heart, mind, and spirit.

Juggling different relationships includes remaining open to others' points of view while establishing trust, and this can create tensions. Staying open and alive to these tensions is part of the job for many of these women, and there are no a priori solutions. Manning (1992) reminds us, "We shouldn't forget that our primary responsibility is to care for. If this means that we are often unsure about just what to do, then we must live with this uncertainty. Discovering what to do requires that we listen carefully to the ones cared for" (p. 53). It takes skill to develop a baby's trust and to build a foundation of trust with staff and parents. With empathy, openness, vulnerability, thought, and experience, caregivers try to see the perspective of the people with whom they work and to appreciate other points of view while maintaining a clear sense of self.

Building trust also requires time: time for reflection, time to connect with infants, and time to meet with other staff members. The best examples of primary caregiving include the time necessary for building relationships.

Primary Caregiving: Focusing on Relationship

In the first interviews, I asked the caregivers about the contrasts between working with preschoolers and infants. All but one of the caregivers had previously worked with preschoolers (ages three years to five years), as well as with children under three years of age. All said they preferred the intimate way of working with the infants because it encouraged deeper relationships. In a recent Canada-wide study on daycare, the authors commented that "ninety-five percent of teachers and nearly as many directors told us that working with children is what keeps them in the job" (Doherty et al., 2000, p. 172).

Lynn preferred the youngest age group to the older group, saying that she had done some work in preschools, but noted, "I definitely prefer infants, then toddlers, then preschool. Preschoolers are just too chatty. They are just too talkative. I like to see them learn the language, learn all those milestones of a one-year-old and then up to a toddler. They are still learning to talk, they are still sweet. I prefer the young ones, the babies." Lynn focused on their "baby-ness" as the important factor in her choice of infants over preschoolers.

Others noted the intimacy of working closely with the same three infants as appealing. Each of these caregivers worked with three babies and their families. Mary said, "Well, I did have a chance to work with the older ones. I guess I really prefer looking after the same three, the primary caregiving, rather than a large group, and you get to know them better, you get to work with the families more personally. It's just more personal; I like that aspect of it."

Others echoed this thought, for example, "The three, that's who you are making connections with, the parents and the child. And three is much easier than a group daycare of twenty-five." Another person commented, "with a bigger group, you can't be as tuned in as you get to be as a primary caregiver." This focus on the same three babies allows an intimacy to develop between caregiver and child.

Mel had just begun working with babies and toddlers and contrasted this with her work with preschool children:

> You have to take their cues and I'm just figuring that out. I kind of knew that before, but it's constant all day long. And everything is so much more flexible with the younger ones. [With preschool children] everything was really school-like, everything was on a schedule and this happened at this time. You actually noticed lots of kids didn't really work that way. Who wants to stop when they're playing? Or they don't sit well or they're just a different type of child. That's what I mostly notice. [In infant care] you have to be really flexible and you have to really be good at reading what's going on, really good at observing where they're at and what they need.

Rachel, when she had worked with preschoolers, was so focused on the program that when she got to work with under-threes, she said, "Wow, finally, I can just let them be who they want to be."

Recently I had a conversation with a practicum student I was teaching who echoed these thoughts. She had begun her professional life as a public school teacher, and according to her, the curriculum was the main focus when you are working with school-age children. When she worked with preschool-age children, she said she was relieved that the curriculum was less important, though the "tradition of school continues with this age group." With babies, she learned about, and enjoyed, following their leads, feeling she had an opportunity to be responsive, truly responsive, to each of their needs. Working with babies moves practice into the realm of the personal, the everyday.

Working closely with three or four infants and their families allows for an intimacy that is challenging to develop within a larger group. The relationship gains depth over time and proximity. Jade said, "For me without the depth, it is shallow, and it doesn't do it for me. It doesn't seem to serve a purpose for me. I need that depth." These women enjoy and nurture the relationships they have; they find satisfaction in being involved with the lives of babies and families. These connections are the reward and the motivation for their work. Perhaps, as the feminist psychologists from the Stone Center suggest, "feeling connected and in contact with another often allows us our most profound sense of personal meaning and reality" (Jordan et al., 1991, p. 289). In that study, Jordan's colleague Surrey emphasizes that for women it "becomes as important to understand as to be understood or 'recognized' by others. It is equally paramount, but not yet emphasized, that women all through their lives feel the need to 'understand' the other—indeed, desire this as an essential part of their own motivating force" (p. 38).

Intimate, close relationships bring these caregivers satisfaction and meaning.

The Relationship with the Baby

In relating to infants, good practice includes responsive caregiving. According to Rachel, the caregiving relationship is "a very reciprocal engagement. They know you are there; you know they are there and yet, they feel they know that they are able to do what their agenda is and when you want something of them, or if they want something of you, you connect." Later she said,

> So much care is nonverbal. Attachment is maybe not demonstrated through language all the time. They are not saying "I love you," but it is about a baby who rolls over to the other side of the room and then quickly glances back at you. And you have in that glance, you are completely connected to them and they are completely connected to you. Then they move on and they go somewhere else. Or, just a glance, or a smile or a quick touch. It may not be a huge moment. It is a huge moment, but it is not a demonstrated, overt moment.

Mel talked of "trust lines" connecting the babies with her. "When you say there is that connection, I have always had that; you know where they are and what they are doing. I visualize an imaginary line connecting you from each one. It sounds weird. It is like a trust line. You can see it. Everyone knows where everyone is, eyes behind your head, that is the feeling."

Relationship is about connection and communication. Connection can elude the visible, and a great deal of communication may be nonverbal. While these qualities are not often quantifiable, they have a deeply felt veracity. To illustrate, Sheryl spoke of each baby's distinct cry:

> Each child has a different cry and different cries for different reasons. For instance, Guy, sometimes his cries are very intense, but the facial expression says something else than a hurt cry; [it] might be a frustrated cry. You have to know the child. That is what is hard when they first come. You don't know them. But once you get to know them, I think, I can gather what a baby needs when he is upset. Sometimes it is just a cry for a toy that is not working for him. Or they cry and look at you. You can say, "I see that you are pretty frustrated," and they are still frustrated, but they keep doing what they are doing. Then there are other cries where they are just learning how to stand up and then all of a sudden it looks as though she wants to sit down and she's been standing for a while and she's stuck. That might be another cry. I'll go, "Are you stuck?" She might want an offer of help or she may want you to know that

she's stuck, but she doesn't want you to help her. Or it could be that she wants you to help her. So I'll offer it to her and see what she does. All cries are different.

Understanding an infant is complex, as his or her personality, style of communicating, and intentions are contributing factors in building relationship. Empathy is necessary. Jade said, "I find it fascinating with the toddlers...some, their language is so expressive....I can just hear...she knows what she is saying, it's not her problem with communication; it is our problem. Because she's got it. I think, how long until we catch up?" Understanding the child's intense desire to communicate, Jade felt it was her responsibility to uncover what was already clear in the child's mind. This level of engagement comes from deep skill and thought; it cannot be ruled by policies or regulations; it cannot be "managed."

It can be frustrating when a caregiver is unable to understand an infant's signals. Caregivers react differently in these situations. Lynn knew that she needed to find out "what works for each one. There are some things that just don't work. It's getting to know the children and what's important to them." Her frustration was palpable when she said:

Okay, I've diapered you, I've fed you, you don't want a drink, so what can I give you? What do I do? One child, in particular, all those needs are met, or to the best we can meet them and they'll sit in your lap and scream. And then they'll start to kick. And you go, well, I don't need to be kicked by you. So I will set you down beside me and you can scream there if you want to. Then they'll just lay down there and kick and scream. Then all of a sudden after five to ten minutes, they have calmed down and we can carry on with what we were doing, which is usually "I'm going to sleep now because I'm exhausted."

On the other hand, Jade said of those moments of frustration, "I try to be quiet and observant, allowing them to explore the world but being there if they need me. I try to follow their agenda. That's what I try to do. I value being mellow, quiet, observant, communicative, but at their need. I would find it really frustrating if I couldn't read their signals. Because they are trying to communicate and I am not getting it. That would feel as though I was not doing it. Like something wasn't right, I'm not getting it."

Lynn's frustration was understandable and many of us who have worked with children can relate to her feelings. Jade had taken another approach, and she felt it her responsibility to understand the baby's communication; if she did not "get it," she continued to puzzle over the failed communication without faulting the baby.

Successfully connecting with the children was a reward for each woman I talked with in this study. Mary said of her relationships with babies, "bonding with them and getting to know them well, I'd have to say that was the best part of it—having the close relationship with them and their parents. It's just more personal." Dawn exclaimed, "I really like the bond that you build. It's incredible!" Jade said the reward is "a feeling. You feel connected and in that connection you can hear each other." Rachel spoke of her special attraction to working with babies, "It's the wonder for me; it's the hope of complete possibilities, like the unknown, the dream and the stars, the relationship, the whole attachment cycle is just so intense."

In its wholeness, a deep relationship with a baby can be both frustrating and rewarding. Lynn said, "There are a lot of frustrating moments, but overall there is the happiness, the joy, the opportunity to watch them grow, to teach them."

While at first glance, caregiving might appear to focus on the relationship with the babies, when looking deeper a web of connection is seen. Sheryl said, "They're not your family. They're not your children. But in the same sense, you are offering them care. There is no fine line, it's sort of like a weaving. There is no straight rule." Obviously, the web of professional caregiving is intricate, with strands connecting from caregiver to the baby and to the other caregivers and the other people in the baby's life. The work of relationship asks caregivers to stay alive to complex and intricate demands. These caregivers must balance the pulls of three babies that may at times be equally strong. Ayers (1993, p. 34) warns that when we accept theory as doctrine, we become "immunized against complexity." Schon (1987) says of the practitioner's world, "in the swampy lowland, messy, confusing problems defy technical solutions" (p. 3). This weaving of relationships creates difficulties that at times defy simple or evident solutions.

Caring for the baby means developing a relationship with the parents, and caring for the baby requires the support of co-workers.

Rachel said that "one of the difficulties is that parental relationship. But the other flip side about it is a real joy for me. I've
worked with parents where it hasn't been a good start, it hasn't
been great, and you have moved past that."

Relationships with Parents

All of the caregivers acknowledged that the connection with parents can be difficult to navigate. Jade said, "You welcome them all
[babies and parents], but they [the parents] are more difficult. Not
difficult, but finding the way to get to it. Parents can be a little bit
more difficult only in that you've got to utilize everything. You've
got to make it work."

Several years ago, Rachel brought primary caregiving into the
toddler setting where she was the supervisor, although her staff was
not convinced that this was a good idea. Over time, she told me,
they found that not only was it easier for the caregivers to relate
more intimately with just four families, but the families themselves
began to interact with each other in a more engaged manner. She
observed, "Those parents immediately connected with the other
parents [within their family grouping], because they knew the other
children. It was easier as they only had to get to know four children." With just four families to relate to, caregivers had the
opportunity to work through difficulties, leading to deeper relationships with the parents than they had experienced previously.
Rachel explained that "before primary caregiving you had a little
tiff with Mrs. Jones and you could just avoid her for a week. You
got someone else to talk to her. But here you can't. You go to her
and she can't avoid you. The bottom line is that eventually you are
going to have to connect with them. You're caring for their child."

Sheryl commented on the ease of talking with just three families "rather than having twenty per day." Enjoying the potential
for deeper contact with each family, she was also clear that "you
connect with them, but you are still the caregiver, not the parent."
She worked with young parents and expressed a desire to find out
more about the experience of being a young parent. She wanted to
more clearly understand "the trials and tribulations of being a
young parent."

Caregivers varied in their approaches to understanding the parental perspectives. Jade saw them as only somewhat challenging. Dawn sought to be, as she says, "respectful to the people I work with and to the children and the moms and caring. I am offering the things I can give, offering the intimacy of myself and my experiences, not that they are right, but just to offer that to them. I try to mother them in some ways." Working in a young mothers' program, Dawn embraced the inherent difficulties by identifying the process as mothering and nurturing. She saw herself as offering support and advice, but tried to maintain an awareness that it might not always be the correct advice.

In caring for babies, the caregivers often cared for the parents. They worked to bring feeling, empathy, and reflection to their relations with parents. They found it important to bring to the task of caring for parents what Ruddick (1989, p. 70) describes as maternal thinking: "feeling, thinking, and action are conceptually linked; feelings demand reflection, which is in turn tested by action, which is in turn tested by the feelings it provokes. Thoughtful feeling, passionate thought, and protective acts together test, even as they reveal, the effectiveness of preservative love."

With regard to the family, Mary simplified issues that might have escalated into a problem: "I haven't really had any major problems with a family. Sometimes you may have a little issue you may not agree on, like sleep patterns and things like that, maybe the child's going to bed too late at night and they want to cut the sleep down to an hour a day and I feel, like hey, that's not enough. We talk it out and compromise." Mary tried to not make issues complicated or to make judgments of the parents; she accepted things as they were and did not take an overly critical view. Such openness welcomed parents since Mary saw issues as sources of discussion toward solution.

Lynn seemed to approach parents carefully, even warily: "Sometimes it can be tough, you've got your primary caregiving groups and you don't know the parents when they start and they are divided into groups and you don't click so well with the ones that you might be primary caregiving with. And that can be a challenge. But you have to slowly get to know these parents. You know the ones you can joke with and the ones you don't dare try to. It just doesn't work."

Feeling uncertain of the parents, Lynn was more comfortable when she was getting positive feedback from the parents. She noted, "We have an excellent group of parents right now. They are so grateful." When parents did not respond to her overtures, she was hurt and uncertain. For example, Lynn did not know how to deal with a mother who had just come out of the hospital with a miscarriage. She said, "I just thought anything I say to her just doesn't go over well. What can you do?" Parents can bring awkward and emotionally fraught situations into the daycare, and caregivers may not have the experience or expertise to deal with their own emotional responses. Co-workers could be a support in these situations. For example, Lynn's teammate said to her, "It was nothing that you said. Don't feel bad. It was just the way she took it. It was her inside feeling just terrible. And she is just coming in to get her daughter and going home."

Relationships with parents are key in the work with small children. A child benefits when her caregiver and her parent can communicate effectively. Like children, adults vary, responding differently to a caregiver's approach and communication. No one single approach works each time and caregivers must be aware and responsive to the individual.

Relationships with Co-workers

When co-workers were supportive, all other relationships seemed to feel easier. There is a tremendous potential for co-workers to create a supportive and nurturing environment for one another. Sheryl said of her teammate, Jade, "We are dancing. We know what we need. Like if I'm working with one child and one of hers comes over, I say, 'Do you want me to give her a snack?' If she agrees, we have a snack together. Whereas [if] a new staff person comes in, they might not know that."

Moving from preschool-age children to working with babies, Dawn spoke of how the support of the staff had helped her as she began her job: "I was really nervous, insecure, I felt really uncomfortable. Because I had some tough moms too, and it was hard. And I thought, 'Have I taken on more than I can chew?' But I had a lot of confidence in the staff; they thought I could do a great job and so it's okay. I could build that confidence through working with people who had that confidence in me and gave me the guidance and skills." She valued learning from her peers "over the last few years, sharing information." She viewed the staff's strengths as complementary: "I think we all share the same philosophy, but all display it in different ways. And then we all are very respectful of people and that comes out in different ways. And we can all bring our experience in different ways, but it all comes out that we respect and care for children and families, that's the biggest picture, the big goal for all of us."

Jade felt it was essential to work together, "because when you're all working together toward the same goal that can become the background and you can really work with what you're working with. But when that doesn't, what should be the easy part becomes the hard part." Jade also talked about the support she received from other members of her team, "It is just getting another perspective or just a reminder that you have done your best. If you are frustrated then you can share that and it's hard, then you can let go of it. Without that I don't know if I could let go of things."

Lynn appeared to miss this staff cohesiveness. In her job, staff relationships have become the difficult part. She spoke urgently and clearly of the differences she had with her co-workers:

> I'm working with two totally different people. One fresh out of high school and just finished the basic ECEC, so you know, just barely twenty. And I'm working with a lady who is a grandma and has raised four children of her own and has two grandchildren. So you have two totally different spectrums and I'm flat center in the middle. So the common goal is that you want the children to be happy and content and have their basic needs met. So yes, we can all see that but how we go about doing that may be different.

Neither of her co-workers had her under-three certificate, so they did not share that common language. Their center had very little time for meetings or communication. Lynn said, "Actually I was thinking just recently about communication and how important it really is when you are working with your fellow staff and sometimes I think, 'oh we're not communicating at all.' That's when things go all hairy and you are ready to go berserk." In any center, having sufficient time to meet and communicate is important (Culkin, 2000).

In the school-based program, with staff hours of 8:30 a.m. to 4:00 p.m., everyone worked the same shift, and thus there was time for staff to meet, to debrief, to connect with each other, and to reflect on the day. When I asked about how staff worked together, Jade acknowledged that everyone was different and that they had different styles, "we come from different places." Keeping the connection between people who have different styles and approaches means "you just keep conversing. There will always be differences but, I think, it can be really exciting to have all differences pooled together to make the greater picture. So when the central goal is similar, differences are good, because it just makes it even bigger."

Mary's program had time to meet, but because the staff worked staggered hours they are unable to meet as often as the school-based program. She said that they all had their own styles of caregiving, "and I know that we don't always agree with each other. We're four different personalities working together, but we have our basic same philosophy toward the children." Despite different personalities, staff members helped each other and Mary worked to understand the other staff members' perspectives. She reflected on how she negotiates her difficulties with another caregiver's practice:

> When a caregiver puts her baby into the nap room and wakes up your baby, and your baby won't go back to sleep, maybe they've only had a twenty-minute nap and they're mad and they want to come out. Eventually, you bring them out, because they're not going back to sleep and then they have a miserable afternoon because they are tired and grumpy and they're clingy. And that can be hard too. You know they need more rest and it didn't work out that time, but it's not the caregiver's fault, so you just deal with it. That happens every now and then. If it happens a lot you try and talk about it. "Maybe you could wait another five minutes till my baby is really settled." That sort of thing could help.

Working together requires cohesion and willing communication; it requires "trust lines" among the staff. Communication demands time and also people who know and are willing to share themselves (Jorde-Bloom, 1988).

Relationship with Self

Working with families and staff, a caregiver needs to have significant self-knowledge. She must understand her needs at many levels and also how to keep herself rested and energized. It takes abundant energy to handle the complexity of this caregiving work. Rachel said, "who the caregiver is defines the care, the core of who the caregiver is." Jade, too, said: "the more balanced you are emotionally and the more you know yourself, the easier it is going to be for you."

On a practical level, the caregivers said that being rested and calm helps with the job of responding to the babies. Both Mel and Mary mentioned eating well as important in maintaining equanimity and energy. Doing tai chi and meditating were also mentioned as useful strategies. All seven women stated that a calm, peaceful atmosphere is necessary. As Mel said, "you don't get all wound up and they won't either."

Jade and Rachel spoke of the importance of understanding yourself at a deeper level. Jade said that "you need to be really flexible. If you have rigidity, this would not be a job for you, because it changes. It is more than just a job; it is with you all the time. More than just the time you put into work." This is not a job that these caregivers did automatically; rather they were involved with people about and for whom they cared. Rachel said, "An awareness, you really have to be self-aware. And maybe it's just to say, 'I know what this trigger is. I know what this feeling is and I'll sit with it. I'm not going to do anything about it.' I know that certain parents trigger me off; I know what triggers me and I react in a way that probably isn't necessarily appropriate. But it's emotion that drives it." Sheryl noted that, "You are always thinking about other ways you could have done it that would be more positive. You continue to think, you always have to be improving yourself." Jade summed it up: "I just do the best with who I am and with who they are."

Empathy, Trust, and Reflection

The caregiver has the responsibility of establishing the relational ground. She is at the center of an enormous, complex web of connections. She must observe and understand her own emotions as well as try to understand and respond to the emotions of babies, parents, and fellow staff. Negotiating this emotional landscape with empathic sensitivity and thought, she uses what Goleman (1998) called "emotional intelligence," "the capacity for recognizing our own feelings and those of others, for motivating ourselves, and for managing emotions well in ourselves and in our relationships" (p. 317). Damasio (1999) suggests that "well-targeted and well-deployed emotions seems to be a support system without which the edifice of reason cannot operate properly" (p. 42).

As Erikson posited, babies develop a sense of trust in their world through their caregivers and the provision of a predictable and responsive world, a world on which they can depend (Erikson, 1950; Lieberman, 1993). Adults as well need trustworthy environments wherein they can be emotionally vulnerable (Kegan, 1982). Working with staff members whom a caregiver trusts can free her to do a better job; her co-workers contribute to the stable ground on which she works. Parents are more relaxed if they are able to depend on their child's caregiver. Here are the "trust lines" that Mel spoke of, and they go not only from the caregiver to the baby, but from baby to caregiver, among the caregivers, between parents and caregiver; they weave a complicated and delicate web.

Trust develops over time. Repeated and consistent interactions lead a baby to conclude that the caregiver will be there to respond to his distress or delights. Over time, staff learns they can count on one another. Through daily contact, parents come to know and understand that the caregiver will be there to support them. Working closely with babies involves a caregiver in an intimate relationship with the children and, hopefully, their families. The time spent in feeding, dressing, and diapering the same baby allows for caregiver and baby to know each other on a familiar level. When the feeding, dressing, and diapering are done with care and attention, the baby can come to trust her caregiver. Rachel explains why inconsistency in caregiving can disrupt a trustworthy environment: "You [the baby] are used to the warm cloth and the little rituals that come with being changed by that person and suddenly you have this other person and you have no idea what they're going to do. You have no control, no predictability, so why would you be emotionally connected to that person? They don't know your cues."

To be responsive and to build trust, caregivers speak of understanding the perspectives of the baby, of the other caregivers, and of the parents. *Webster's Collegiate Dictionary*, 7th edition, (1965) defines *empathy* as the "capacity for participating in another's feelings or ideas." Trying to uncover the parents' feelings and thoughts and trying to find the baby's perspective are of concern to the caregiver. Goleman (1998) points to empathy as one of the ways people monitor their own and others' emotions, and asserts that empathy can help guide thought and action.

Looking after babies can be thought of as a series of tasks to be accomplished, which suggests caregiving to be a series of tasks with the focus on task completion rather than on the baby. In responding to a baby, a caregiver must act empathetically, trying to feel into the baby's perspective, and emotions. The caregiver thus has not only a list of tasks to complete, but the meta-task of monitoring both the baby's emotions and her own and doing those tasks in a manner congruent with her empathic understanding. The renowned pediatrician and child psychiatrist, D. W. Winnicott is quoted in Shepherd, Jones, and Robinson (1996) as saying, "When I myself started, I was conscious of an inability in myself to carry my natural capacity for empathy with children back to include empathy with babies. I was fully aware of this as a deficiency, and it was a great relief to me when gradually I became able to feel myself into the infant-mother or infant-parent relationship. I think that many who are trained in the physical side must do the same sort of work in themselves in order to become able to stand in a baby's shoes" (p. 40).

Jade, who believes empathetic reflection to be essential, said, "You get a perspective on yourself, on who you are working with. There are so many facets—to the whole picture. If it was just you and your reaction, you have a limited picture. It's about you and the mood you are in that day, or the mood they are in that day. It is pretty limiting. But if you can keep open to see the whole thing, then you let go and start again the next day." Both Dawn and

Sheryl echoed Jade as Dawn said it was important to look at things from "a wholly different aspect," while Sheryl said one must see another's point of view so that "work or life becomes easier."

Mel described how she connected with a fifteen-month-old who was new to her program:

> I sit back and watch and I wait for them to feel okay; I wait for them to be familiar with me. Then you kind of establish a connection with them. You are both aware of each other. This week one of the children I cared for had no connection in the daycare at all. She had never been in daycare before and she was very attached to her mom and her dad. It is heartbreaking to watch when her mom leaves. She wants to be all by herself and cry and cry and cry. I know I don't want to go over there and invade her space, because obviously she doesn't want to have anything to do with anything and [so] last week I would sit by her and be close to her. I wouldn't touch, I would let her know I was there and gradually, ohhh-hh, every day it was like.... There is nothing I could do to make her okay with anything; then, gradually, she came to me one day and ever since then she has an awareness of where I am and where she is. That is basically what I did; I observed.

I would suggest that, in addition to observation, she was also aware of this child and her feelings, in such a manner that the child felt her awareness and her caring. We can be present to others so that it is palpable.

The Dalai Lama (Lama and Cutler, 1998) speaks of empathy as a route to compassion, saying, "One can attempt to increase compassion by trying to empathize with another's feeling or experience" (p. 89). Empathizing and developing compassion can be arduous journeys, with observation a beginning toward understanding. Children learn by watching the world around them and caregivers learn about an individual child by observing closely. An infant may be nonverbal, but she is communicating; an observant caregiver learns about an infant by being fully present to her. Paying attention to a baby's signals or cues and learning to understand the messages takes time, careful observation, and being fully focused in the present moment. Agreeing with Mel, Rachel felt strongly that observing is the key to knowing the infant. She stated, "Observing! Being fully present for the infant. They know you are there. Being fully present to me means that I'm there and completely allowing them to do what they are capable of doing in that environment."

The Catholic theologian Henri Nouwen (1975) writes of the healing that is possible with "the full and real presence of people to each other" (p. 95). Echoing Rachel's acceptance of the infants in the moment, he writes, "Really honest receptivity means inviting the stranger into our world on his or her terms, not on ours." The practice of being fully present opens up possibilities of reciprocal connection for both people. Miller and Stiver (1997) call "mutual empathy...the great unsung human gift" (p. 29).

Gerber (1979) also describes being present for a baby through what she refers to as "wants nothing" quality time. Here, the caregiver "has no plans other than wanting simply to be with the child...being there with all the senses awakened to the child." She believes that too often in our culture children feel they must produce something to keep an adult's attention. Instead, being present "thinking only of the child" is a "peaceful presence—a quiet assurance in this beingness" (p. 21).

A colleague of Nouwen's, Parker Palmer (1983) speaks of receptivity to another: "I will try to respond to your feelings with an understanding that comes from knowing my own" (p. 85). An awareness of one's own feelings is involved in coming to understand another's feelings. Through understanding a child's point of view, a caregiver can carry awareness into action.

Mary spoke of her own response to understanding the perspective of one of her young toddlers:

> Right now I have a little girl [fifteen months], she's a very sensitive girl and she doesn't like me to disappear into the kitchen because she can't see me or I'm going to the bathroom with another child. She always wants me right there in the same room and then she has the confidence to get up and play, as long as I don't go too far. What I've started doing with her is when it's time to go into the kitchen and make the snack—that seems to be a time of anxiety for her. Now I'll just say to her that you can come along with me, and I sit her in the chair in the kitchen and give her her juice and she will watch me make the snack. Then I will bring her out and the snack together and

it seems to be working. But often I'll just have to get the other
staff to prepare something for me in the kitchen.

Not only did Mary understand what the child was feeling, she
acted on her knowledge and reassured the girl by not leaving her
behind. She varied her responses to each child depending on their
signals and needs. She explained, "I know which ones can go off
and run and play and I know which ones need to sit on my lap for
ten minutes and feel comfortable enough, that I'm not going to
leave them." Over time, as caregivers combine experience with
observation, they are able to respond appropriately in a shorter
time. Jade said, "You can get more quickly to what your response
might be, because after eleven years there is only so many things it
could be with a baby. So you kind of get a repertoire." Experience
makes it easier to tune into what might be happening for an infant.

Learning to listen to other people helps caregivers discern and
sort through their own feeling and thoughts. Caregivers develop a
broader view as they incorporate others' viewpoints. Dawn says,
"It's a struggle all the time. Because I think we all care about children and stuff, it's all our own values, my personal values are
always triggered, but my values are not somebody else's values and
that is the biggest thing I try to remember."

The approach of these caregivers is typical of connected
knowers; "connected knowers learn through empathy" (Belenky et
al., 1986, p. 115). They "enter into the perspectives of others
through empathic role-taking processes that draw on feelings, narratives, and the particulars of personal experience" (Belenky,
Bond, and Weinstock, 1997, p. 61). Many of the caregivers talk of
trying to understand the parents to whom they relate and the
babies for whom they care. Jade said she tried to know "where
they are at and follow their leads." Understanding the point of
view requires both feeling and thought. As Belenky et al. say,
"Connected knowing involves feeling, because it is rooted in relationship: but it also involves thought" (p. 121).

An empathic relationship is dynamic, requiring "time and
energy and thought" (Kaplan, 1995). One must approach the
other person actively and take on his or her set of beliefs and
values, while not necessarily adopting them. Josselson (1995)
says that "empathy is premised on continuity, recognizing that

kinship between self and other offers an opportunity for a deeper and more articulated understanding" (p. 31). Dawn said of the young mothers she works with, "I have some skills that I can offer them and they are in a different place in their life than I am. But I am also not going to be their parent and tell them this is how you have to do it. I have to respect where they are at and follow their leads."

Gilligan and Wiggins (1988) speak of "the affective imagination" as drawing on the "ability to enter into and understand through taking on and experiencing the feelings of others" (p. 120). Jordan et al. (1991) claim that empathy involves both affective and cognitive functioning and is a "complex, developmentally advanced and interactive process" (p. 120). Empathy fosters growth and it is in empathetic connection that deeper knowledge of another is gained. Jordan et al. affirm Ruddick's (1989) claim that "feelings demand reflection, which is in turn tested by action, which is in turn tested by the feelings it provokes" (p. 70). This is the hermeneutic circle of thought, feeling, and action.

Dahlberg et al. (1999) suggest that a discourse of meaning-making is central in a postmodern world of diverse understandings. I would add that empathy and reflection are an integral aspect of this discourse of meaning-making, cultivating "the ability to see the Other as equal but different and the capacity to reverse perspectives" (p. 109). Mature empathy recognizes that the other person in her wholeness has another perspective. Sheryl showed interest in going to a conference about young parents because "I haven't lived their experience and I think I would like to understand more the trials and tribulations of being a young parent."

Miller and Stiver (1997) speak of empathy as "resonating and responding" (p. 44). They say that "children need to learn about their own thoughts and feelings, and in order to do that they need others who can be mutually empathic with them, can resonate with them and respond to them" (pp. 44–45). Being in relationship with empathic, caring people helps children begin to experience the richness of their emotions and to articulate them.

Taking on another's perspective does not indicate the surrender of one's own. As Clinchy (1996) wrote, "Without self-knowledge we cannot exploit genuine similarities between self and other, using 'templates' in the self to guide us to 'matches' in the other"

(p. 230). Awareness of feelings moves from within, yet is directed outward. Mary was aware of her centrality in the emotional transactions that occurred each day and knew to keep herself focused and rested: "I have my energy and my rest and I am relaxed and then I feel I can do anything. The hard part is if I haven't had a good sleep I am talking to myself all day getting myself through every little caregiving routine, making sure they are okay. Also dealing with parents and making sure they are okay."

Sheryl spoke of saying good-bye to a child in her care. She was aware of her feelings and was responsible for them, able to speak of her feelings within the larger context of a "natural progression" as well as acknowledging the feelings of the child and parent: "But eventually he will move over to the toddler side, I might not go with him, but that is the natural progression. I'll feel sad about it, but I'll let the mom know and I'll let Sam know, but it is not something that will ruin my life or their life. It's just sadness."

The caregiver has the responsibility of establishing the relational ground monitoring and managing her own emotions, while attempting to understand and respond to the emotions of babies, parents, and fellow staff. Negotiating this emotional landscape with empathic sensitivity and thought, she is always in need of her emotional intelligence.

Chapter 7

Hearing from the Caregivers

The first time I interviewed Mary, whom I did not know well, I felt that she was not as engaged in our interview as were the other participants. Soon, I was not engaged either. A small, egocentric voice inside me was muttering, "Why isn't she interested in my questions?" I began to feel sleepy. Fortunately, I had another small voice curious about why this was happening. I was intrigued and I wondered what was actually occurring. I pushed through my first reactive thoughts and my sleepiness, cleared my mental obstacles, paid attention, and heard a cue from her that led me to ask the right question. She had recently found out she was pregnant and was thrilled. At that point, few people knew and, of course, it was taking up her thoughts. She was less involved in the external world while her internal world was changing and evolving. My judgmental voice was not useful, but my curious voice was.

After several close readings of the interview transcripts, I realized that besides uncovering dimensions of caregiving, I was also seeing four distinct frames for practice from the most experienced of the caregivers I interviewed. Each woman viewed caregiving from a different perspective, representing aspects of caring—intellectual, sensual, practical, and spiritual. As thoughtful, careful caregivers, each responded to the challenge of caregiving in her unique style. The other three caregivers also illustrated aspects of caring, less dramatic, but no less important.

Mary: Knowing Self

Mary had worked with babies for ten years in the work-site center that had been her practicum placement as a student, but her experience with other age groups and settings was limited. The program and staff had supported her as she matured into a thoughtful caregiver. During these years, she learned about herself and her own rhythms and while this might appear obvious, not everyone develops this self-awareness. Knowing herself, her own rhythms, her own energy levels, she was better able to have a balanced and consistent relationship with babies and families while maintaining her own balance (Yelland, 2000).

To be in a healthy relationship with other people requires having a healthy relationship with one's self. Self-awareness means having "an inner representation of a self that is doing this in relation to other selves" (Jordan et al., 1991, p. 17). When I asked Mary what she had learned from her work over the years that she had not learned in school, she answered:

> Wow, I guess it is learning to deal with yourself. I guess there is a little bit of that in the [ECEC] program, but certainly over the years working here I have learned how much better to deal with my own stress and be a lot more relaxed. I know they talk about that a bit. That has been a big one for me. My first few years I would need every sick day that I had and I would be tired all the time and I guess now I can just be more objective and not get caught up in everything. I have a lot more energy.

Some of what Mary had learned may sound simple, but this learning is often difficult to enact. She paid attention to taking care of herself physically, saying, "You need support systems and you do need breaks. You need lots of rest, you need to keep yourself healthy and you need to eat well. That is where your stamina comes from. You need lots of exercise and fresh air. You need all these things. It is such a demanding job. It is very enjoyable as well, but you know the main thing is you need to have the energy for these children because if you don't have that you are not being fair to them. They need that from you, they deserve that."

Mary talked in terms of physical well-being, but her reasoning spoke of her commitment to children. Children deserve good care;

they deserve a caregiver who is at her best. She set high standards
for herself. When she was relaxed, so were the babies. She said,
"they certainly read our reactions and emotions very well." Parker
Palmer says, "self-care is never a selfish act—it is simply good
stewardship of the only gift I have, the gift I was put on earth to
offer others" (2000, p. 30).

At first, Mary found the work difficult and "would get stressed
out pretty easily." She was nineteen when she began, and worked
with women who were older. She observed the other staff and
found that they would help her and give her support. Now she
conducts herself with a sense of confidence that helps to put parents at ease, empathizing with parents' difficulty as they begin day
care with their baby, saying:

> I try to be there, you know, open and flexible. If they have any
> questions I always say when they start, "Any time you want to
> talk about anything give me a call, or we can arrange a meet-
> ing." At first they are not too sure about how I am going to be,
> because I look so young and inexperienced. Now that I have
> been here for this many years, a lot of them are feeling, "It's
> okay, she'll be all right. My baby will be all right." We usually
> have pretty good relationships. I try to make them feel comfort-
> able. I have a certain way of introducing them to the center and
> we talk about how I am going to make their baby feel much
> more comfortable with doing routines the same way they do.
> When they first start they know what comes next and that puts
> them at ease, and I think knowing that they can phone or come
> by any time really helps them too.

Mary discussed self-care as critical to her understanding of and
coping with her job. Focusing on herself and her emotional and
physical needs, she has learned to understand and trust herself.
Other caregivers with whom I spoke have echoed her thoughts
about self-care.

Understanding of self and how to care for one's self is essential
in being able to form and maintain good relationships. Mahoney
(1996) said, "presence with others both requires and deepens a
presence with self" (p. 134). Caregivers who use this opportunity
to deepen their sense of themselves gain a confidence, a security,
in relating to families and babies; they have a self to share with

others rather than being dependent on others to define them (Kegan, 1982).

Being self aware and knowing how to keep working at one's best requires experience and a mindful attitude. Awareness of physical needs extends to knowledge of what one needs on the mental, emotional, and spiritual levels as well.

Rachel: Always Learning

Echoing a number of Mary's thoughts, Rachel (another experienced caregiver) said, "I remember when I first started I had this feeling in my stomach, you know, I don't know what to do, I don't know what to do! And then eventually you learn to trust yourself and you learn to read your own cues."

Rachel had spent the last few years substituting and working in different settings as she balanced work with going to school. She worked at the college-based program that supported her return to get her BA in Child and Youth Care. She had done several Resources for Infant Educarers training courses and had spoken locally to caregivers about Magda Gerber's (1979) philosophy and work. In the field for seventeen years, she had worked with infants and toddlers for ten years, gaining a variety of experiences working in infant centers. Despite her different field experiences, she says "the core of how I react to children is still the same."

During our discussions Rachel commented on the length of time (over ten years) she has worked with children, "It is really hard for me to think it was that long. For me, it's not that long, because each time I learned something new it was like a completely new experience for me." Each new job offered her new information and new knowledge. At different points, she took another course or workshop that would give her even more on which to reflect. "I think that what really transformed me was the second year of my early childhood education [training], my special needs and under-threes courses. That really shifted the focus for me."

It was with the infant-toddler course that Rachel found the work that truly called to her. While taking her infant-toddler course she began to work in a toddler program where "I was able to take theory and just apply it right into practice and I had good modeling...so that was good." She had enjoyed working with preschool children, but with the toddlers she found there was "a spark." With this age group she felt comfortable and she loved "their energy and wonder." She went on to take her Resources for Infant Educarers training and found "the spark was even brighter for me with infants."

She continued with a focus on under-threes, taking workshops in RIE with Magda Gerber and working in the field with this age group. Eventually she felt she needed to continue her post-secondary education: "I felt something was missing for me. And I needed to go back and do more theory."

Going back to the university, Rachel was exposed to further theories and ideas. With her years of practice, she could examine these theories in light of her experiences. She began to see "how theory fits in with practice." Before she "never took the time" and now she had the time to read and think. She was developing a critical stance; she examined theories from a different perspective. She alternated between theory and practice, saying it was important for her to "go back and forth between them [theory and practice]. You really have to have the two to get the whole picture. For me, I do."

Her experience in the university had given her a wider perspective and she felt that she "is coming from a different base now. Now I'm observing more and I'm seeing different things. I'm just really enjoying the knowledge and being able to apply the knowledge. Beyond application now to critiquing, saying 'I don't know if I really buy that whole thing' or 'Oh, my gosh, it's really true!'" She said she could now discuss issues on an "extended level" and had had a chance to examine the research in her field.

Rachel had an opportunity in her program to look more deeply at the theories and skills of child care, such as issues of attachment, cultural influences, and interpersonal communication. She had had an opportunity to question and reflect on herself and her own beliefs. Discussing attachment and the importance of acknowledging a child's leave taking she looked at her own practice and had found an area for scrutiny,

> Yes, there are rituals to saying good-bye [to children leaving the program]. We always give them a little book and give the mom a little gift. We always get to choose the book because

you know what the child and parent would appreciate and that type of thing. And I began to realize I always schedule an early day for that day or like I'll make lunches or do something like that so that I don't have to deal with the actual good-byes. When the parents come in in the morning, I'll say my good-byes to them then.... So now I'm thinking, "So what's behind that?"... Now I have the opportunity to deeply reflect on it and... [I found]... in our family, it was always encouraged to never look back.

Rachel went on to discuss her understanding of patterns that worked at one point in her life and her growing awareness of the limitations they placed on her in providing good care for the babies in her care. Self-knowledge grew with her integration of theoretical knowledge.

When she went back to the university, she was wondering if she should try another type of work since she had been caregiving for so long. However, she commented, "Now I've finished and I've realized that that's my total heart and passion [working with babies and toddlers]. I can see myself not necessarily working in day care until I'm sixty-five, I mean physically, I don't think I could do it. But, mentally and in my heart, I know that I will always be with babies or with toddlers."

Education had been a way for her to keep focused on her passion, keeping alive her relationship with her practice. Within this relationship, Rachel had continued to grow and learn; mind and heart informed each other and theory and practice were intertwined. She is a reflective practitioner in the sense of Schon (1991, p. 5), as she "reflect[s] on the understandings already built into the skillful actions of everyday practice." Viewing new experiences and education as a way to keep learning and reflecting on her practice, Rachel has kept her love of the work alive and dynamic.

Dawn: Dealing with the Sensual

Dawn had been at the *school-based program* for seven years, bringing with her experiences with other age groups and in other settings. Speaking with her hands and her face alight, Dawn described the softness and the physicality of infants.

Though other caregivers mentioned the physical dimension of the work, Dawn stressed it. Babies must be touched to be changed and fed. To feel loved and cared for, they need to be touched (Carlson, 2005). As Reite (1990) has written, "Touch appears to be an important part of the initial establishment of attachment bonds, especially in young organisms" (p. 218). As Ashley Montagu (1971) tells us, the skin covers us like a "cloak" and is "the first medium of communication." While touch is important to all of us, we often ignore it, yet the nonverbal and intuitive information that we receive from our sense of touch arrives constantly. Greenough (1990) notes, "we can deprive an animal of most sound and all vision, but how do you deprive an animal of touch?" (p. 119).

Touch and the sensuous aspects of the practice seemed to frame much of Dawn's thinking about her work. She said, "The tactile carries so much emotion and experience through our fingers and our bodies. We carry so much energy through our bodies to touch other people; it's amazing what you can heal and soften." This is similar to Jean Vanier's (1998) comment, "When we begin to listen to our bodies, we begin to listen to reality through our own experiences, we begin to trust our intuition, our hearts" (p. 25).

Dawn liked the softness of the babies; not only their physical softness, but their openness to the world, as contrasted with older children "where the older kids get so manipulated by society, school, and that sort of stuff." Images of softness and contact abounded in my discussions with her: she used the word "softness" often and words like "intimacy," "mothering," "heal and soften," and "feel right."

Babies need touch and we need to touch them. The fear of the accusation of child abuse has silenced us regarding the pleasures and power of touch (Farquhar, 2000; Tobin, 1997). Touch is the only directly reciprocal sense we have, the sense that when we touch someone, we know they feel it and we feel it. Abram (1996) reminds us that "to touch is also to feel oneself being touched, that to see is also to feel oneself seen" (p. 69).

Dawn learned she needed to "go slow"; in a sense, she needed to gentle her tempo in response to babies. She said she would tell someone entering the field that "you learn as you go along and trust in yourself and slow down." She spoke of the "dance of caring" for the baby and the parents. Throughout our discussion Dawn used words like "dance" or "a little dance." She spoke of infants learning "by the feel, by their instincts" and of the "push-pull" of the work. Physical metaphors abounded in Dawn's conversation: "I love the movements, the eye contacts, the growing. Wow, I can have a hand in helping to develop caring and love. I think it starts so early and that's what I really love about it."

Trusting in her own body and its knowledge, Dawn's awareness of her sensual perceptions heightened her awareness of the sensuality of the infants. Her own emphasis on touch and movement was echoed in the babies and their explorations of the world. She said, "The infants are learning social skills, like touching and feeling, and doing the instinctual stuff. The younger ones are just learning by the feel, by their instincts, they don't get impressions from society yet, saying how to do things, it's more inner." She felt she resonated with and understood a baby's approach to the world.

Her own sensitivity to emotions was expressed physically. She felt her emotions intensely. Talking openly of the sadness she experienced watching children leave, she said, "It's very hard to say good-bye. I'm always bawling." Tension was something felt and expressed. She said about the babies: "They feel so much that if there is a tension between the mother and the caregiver the baby feels that. It will transfer from the mother, as well as from me."

Dawn was aware of her own sensuality, and she trusted the information that she received through touch and her other senses. She acknowledged listening to both her body and mind in her work. When I asked if she preferred infants or toddlers she said, "I think at different times I prefer one group or the other. It depends on where my body is at or my mind is at." She connected with both parents and babies through touch. Working with young mothers she has found that she can communicate more fully with a mom when there is a physical connection, for example, a hand on her arm or a hug when needed. She explained that "It is hard to let your mind wander and go somewhere else when you're connected at the physical level. So for me, that is the place I know I'm touching them, because you've got that body connection, as well as the mind connection. Someone's mind can't be wandering, because they're connected to you. It's the same with children. Touch their feet, or anywhere."

Within our North American culture there is, at the moment, a fear of touching young children and a distrust of those who might touch them. But Dawn advocates and speaks to the value of touching children, because children benefit and so does the caregiver. Silin (1997) argues that "the road to combating moral panics... begins with knowing about the importance of touch in early care settings" (p. 231). The world of the senses is important to Dawn. Aware of connecting with others through the metaphors of touch, she also used touch to make literal connections. Dawn felt that touch for young children created a sense of safety, "our world, our space is so big, that kind of closeness brings it together, it's safe. It brings safety into it." Adults need to feel safe also. Aware of this need for herself, Dawn found that the team helped make the space secure for her, "the team makes it safe for me."

When work was too overwhelming for Dawn, she shares, "I talk about it with the staff. I do a lot of talking about it. And I've learned to let it go where I work. There is a little ritual I do in the car and I kind of let it all go and I release my body. I still think about it, but I let the heavy stuff go."

Through her senses, Dawn had experienced and enjoyed the children. Her sensual appreciation had attuned her to the needs of the children. She expressed the meaning she found in the work through a physical metaphor:

> I really like the bonds that you build. It's incredible. It's so amazing, especially if you are able to work with a child for two years; the attachment that happens is just amazing [the one] that you build with the child and the family. It's very strong. It's sad to see them go. That whole feeling of unconditional caring and love and knowing that, you know, if I can give him a really neat touch during the day at some point they'll remember that one touch and maybe teach them that life is really cool... or something.... Even if I gave them that feeling of a special place, a feeling of warmth. That's neat.

Oxenhandler (2001) has written about the dilemma of "touching" in the *Eros of Parenthood*, as has Tobin (1997) in *Making a Place for Pleasure in Early Childhood Education*. Dawn, along with these two authors, challenges us to openly acknowledge the pleasure of physical contact with children and acknowledge the wisdom of our bodies.

Too often the physical body is ignored. Yet it is through our bodies that we learn about the world and each other. All the caregivers agreed that the physical closeness of working with infants was enjoyable. Jade says, "the favorite part of my job is cuddling with the babies," while Rachel describes the touching of babies as being about hands. "Hands. Everything is about that. I'm going to pick you up, I'm going to feed you, I'm going to give you a bottle, I'm going to diaper you, I'm going to sit with you, I'm going to hold you. It's hands."

Jade: Philosophy and Intuition

In her tenth year at the school-based center, Jade had worked the longest of all the caregivers with both babies and older children. She had evolved a particularly philosophical and spiritual approach to her work. Her philosophy of life permeated her discussion of babies. Believing that each child had something to teach her, Jade worked hard to connect with each one.

We spoke of how she had felt when she first worked with babies and how she was feeling at the beginning of her tenth year, and she commented:

> I find it quite different now than when I first started. When I first started it was a discovery: not knowing and trying to figure it out. But I think with not having had a lot of experience it was really hard to figure out what it was I wasn't getting; whereas now I feel much more confident. There's a variety of things you can go for and you can usually find it pretty easily. If it's being wrapped up tight in a blanket or it's not being wrapped up tight in a blanket. Different temperatures in a bottle, the distraction of other people—there're certain things now that are really clear. There's this baby I have now that it's obvious that he's so sensitive. The texture of the rug, when he rolls off the blanket, bothers him. Other babies' cries bother him, so he's just real sensitive. I think in the past it would have taken me a long time; they all look the same. I wouldn't have known which was which, but now I think I am getting it and it has only been a week or two . . . [since she has had this very sensitive baby].

I had observed her with the baby she is describing and have included the observation here, as it illustrates so well what Jade was saying. Comparison was not the purpose of the observations, but I had especially noted this baby and had asked Jade about him.

> From my journal, October 6, 1999. (Ra is eight months old).
>
> Ra goes to Jade fussing. Jade explains she will put Sal down and get Ra's blanket for him. She puts Sal down and goes to get Ra's blanket and bottle. "Ra, here's your blanket. I have your bottle. You know what that means."
>
> She wraps him up in the blanket and then drapes a cloth around his face as she rocks in the rocker and feeds him a bottle. He is quiet and peaceful.
>
> ASIDE: Jade explained to me that she had noticed that Ra liked to feel things. He rubbed his face, hands, head on many different textures; he loved to roll up in the sheepskin. When he went to sleep he liked to have a cloth in his hand and rub it on his face. One time he had a terry cloth bib on and she went to get a baby who had woken up and so she said, "I will get so-and-so and be back to feed you." She came back to see he had fallen asleep with the bib pulled over his face. Now she wraps him as he likes to feel snug, and then she drapes a cloth around the side of his face. She likes to see his face as he falls asleep. She had observed all of this in the first two weeks.

As all the other caregivers did, Jade focused on the relationships: "You want to make this connection, make it work...I think it gets easier to do over the years." She went on to say that the connection "goes both ways. Once you have that connection, you are getting all this stuff. It's definitely not one-sided." In a similar vein, the philosopher and theologian Jean Vanier (1998) says that "the process of teaching and learning, of communication, involves movement, back and forth: the one who is healed and the one who is healing constantly change places" (p. 25).

Miller and Stiver (1997) speak of "mutual empathy": each participant in a relationship contributes "at a different level of empathy based on her/his age and experience, but each can be fully engaged in their shared activity and this action advances each person's psychological development" (p. 44). Speaking with Jade regarding children with whom it is difficult to connect, she said,

I think it is your personality, their personality, the child and the whole bigger picture. But *difficult* is a funny word. It is difficult only in that you have to find a way that takes more energy than another child for you, because this is something you need to work with. But I wouldn't take one child and say, "This is an extremely difficult child for anyone." That is not necessarily the case. It might be a difficult one for you and quite easy for someone else. Think of a high-pitched scream that might bounce off the walls and may not bother someone else at all. And that may be the one thing that is hard for you to deal with. Maybe some other little thing that a child does drives them crazy [but] doesn't bother you at all. So difficulty is according to the person, I think.

Counting on experience to help her connect, Jade also paid more attention to her intuition and her sense of the dimensions beyond the verbal. She was open to hearing what a child or family might tell her beyond the words of conversation. Regarding intuition, she said,

I think the more you know yourself and the more open you are the more open the channel is for that to come through. I'm not really sure of the source of it, but I think the more cluttered you are with your own stuff, the less able you are to use it. I think everyone has it. But not everyone can utilize it or believe in it or trust it. Years ago, I think that was where I was at. Now it's like, it has worked for me enough times that I am quite confident I don't have to figure it out. When it comes, I'll go with it, because it usually is right, if it is a flow.

She felt that accumulated experience strengthens intuition; "it sits there and I can probably tap into more of my intuition based on accumulated experience than I could have done at one time." Looking more closely at the notion of intuition, Jade said, "Where does it come from? Philosophically, I don't know if it's from a greater source and you are just more open to let it through. Does that make sense?" Jade trusts a process that is based on knowing herself, her experience, and her emotional memory (Goleman, 1998); she has transcended the "rational" for a process she has difficulty naming. Or as Damasio (1999) suggests, we cannot make rational decisions without knowing our emotions.

Jade has not thought in terms of generalities and judgments, but rather in terms of deeper, broader, more philosophical meanings. She has wondered how what she does fits into a greater scheme, and what meanings particular difficulties have in her life. Working to connect with her babies and her parents, she remained aware that her efforts may not always succeed. For example, she said,

> There is always something there that you can connect to [in a baby or parent]...there is always something. So to me, if you can't find that something then maybe you shouldn't be in the realm of that person's reality. Because there is always something. The challenge is to find it. It's kind of sad when you don't, but then it's okay, but you think, okay, maybe it's not for you to be the key to open the door...there are lots of people in the world, maybe someone else is the key. You've got to believe that or it will be too sad.

At times, Jade realized that she must assume roles that did not fit comfortably to accomplish her goals. She preferred to let relationships unfold, but one year she was faced with a rapid succession of babies and mothers:

> One of the things, for me, that I have learned, because every year has brought its own lessons, and, I think, there was a year or two that there was a lot of turnover for me in moms and children and staff. It just kept on and I kept thinking, "What is this about?" To attach and have to let go each day was really hard. But I finally came to the conclusion that it's about life—life is too short to take too long to make the attachment. And I realized I might only have a short time and I want to be as effective as I can. So I learned to move the attachment much faster, so that if they're only here a month, at least, there's something there, like I'm not going to take my time and sit back and wait because I might not be able to have the time to make an attachment.

Each situation and relationship has offered a lesson and its own opportunity to develop wisdom, to which Jade has tried to remain open. Being open means to remove the "clutter" of "your own stuff." This is similar to Palmer's (1983) and Nouwen's (1975) notions of hospitality and welcoming other people with openness; each child, student, client comes with a gift and a promise that can be missed if not attended to (Palmer, 1983). Jade remained open and receptive to each encounter and the lessons embedded therein. She would agree that the babies and families are "like guests who honor the house with their visit and will not leave it without having made their own contribution" (Nouwen, 1975, p. 89).

Jade's belief that she is there to "make a difference" has guided her. It has been a tricky balance, "because it is the whole big picture and the immediate moment to moment. And I think the balance of that takes a long time to get." How one feels at the end of the day can alert her to being in or out of balance. Jade supports Nouwen's observation that "to help, to serve, to care, to guide, to heal, these words were all used to express a reaching out toward our neighbor whereby we perceive life as a gift not to possess but to share" (Nouwen, 1975, p. 109) when she says:

> Do you feel like you're frustrated or do you feel like you have put in a good day—that you have accomplished something—not in a task way—but has the day been a bit better along the way for someone because of who you are and what you've put into the day? So if you've had a lot of days where that isn't happening, then I'd really have to look at, "Hey, I think I'm missing the big picture." When you get the big picture, I think, you do get that…that you did what you could. Every time I say that, it sounds like I'm task oriented and it's not that. Like, if you could give out in the day, and feel okay for yourself at the end of the day for what you've given out of yourself; if your day has all been full of negativity or anger or judgment then you're not going to feel good at the end of that day. And sometimes you do need the debriefing with the staff to get rid of all that stuff so you can start the next day feeling good. That's the now. The bigger picture is that it makes a difference in the long run, that you make a difference in this world, somehow. That's the real big picture. That your life makes a difference to the world. But that's so big.

Over the years from her experience, Jade has developed a philosophy of work that fits in with a philosophy of life. Mary, Dawn, and Rachel have all reflected over time and developed their own unique understandings of their work. The other three were as articulate and thoughtful, but with less experience with babies, were more tentative in their thoughts.

Sheryl: "Staying Calm"

Sheryl has her BA in Child and Youth Care and, at the time of this study, had recently finished her practicum for her under-three certificate. She had a wide variety of experiences with children, and recently, had been working with children with diverse abilities. Although at her present job for less than a year, she had had experience with babies in other settings. Her first experience with primary caregiving had been distressing, and she was not an advocate of the RIE philosophy (Gerber and Johnson, 1998) until her present job. She had worked in a center that had followed the RIE philosophy and had concerns and questions of what they did. She explained that:

> I was just asking and questioning, like "why do you believe that?" They wouldn't give an answer that would really fit with what I had in mind. For instance, I know when I worked there they would put the babies to sleep. If they cried you weren't supposed to pick them up, because you knew they were tired. So you would have babies in the sleep room with other babies that were already sleeping, wailing away and they didn't want you to pick up this child. And to me, this was just heartbreaking. So I would ask and ask and I guess they got tired of that. And then they would say, we don't do things to babies they can't get out of themselves, like [strapping them into] highchairs, or the strollers or whatever, but they would wrap the babies up to hold them in their blankets. I said, well, aren't you going against what you believe in, because you're wrapping them up, they can't get out of the blanket. They couldn't explain that.

When Sheryl left that job they told her she wasn't suited to the work, which was "heartbreaking, because I really enjoyed working with the babies." Fortunately, she found that not all centers were the same. She found places where she was comfortable and said, "I felt I could be myself and I wasn't walking on eggshells. I could just do it. I would still watch the other people caregiving, but I felt so much more comfortable, so much more okay—I am caregiving!"

Sheryl thought about the interactions she saw and the discussions she had, and asked questions. During our discussions as I interviewed her she would ask me questions, and I always looked forward to them. When I went to her center, the school-based program, to observe, she would share the thoughts she had had since our previous discussion. On November 17, I noted that Sheryl had been thinking about the nature of the attachment that a caregiver has with an infant. She wondered if we could call it "professional attachment." We discussed ideas concerning attachment and wondered how one might differentiate between the attachment a parent has and the attachment a caregiver has. Eventually, she dismissed the discussion with "it all becomes wordplay." Sheryl was interested in what appeared to work. At university she had found that "there was so much theory, what you see on paper and what you actually do may be two different things." She found she could not work from a chosen theory, what has guided her has been "what works for you and that is what you go for."

As Mary has, Sheryl has taken a pragmatic approach to care for babies. She mentioned several times, "I try to be calm with the kids" or "I stay calm by knowing that I'm doing the best that I can." This, of course, is not easy at times when two babies simultaneously needed attention. She has known that staying calm is ultimately calming for the babies, stating, "I have to be more realistic of what I can do. Not do everything at once and take one step at a time."

Echoing Mary, Sheryl has been defining and discovering her own needs to maintain balance. As Dawn has found, Sheryl knew she had to slow down and relax. She said, "I think that sometimes if you're not conscious of it, if you do try to meet everyone's needs at the same time, you're so anxious about meeting everyone's needs that they become anxious; so why not relax, so they can relax?"

Lynn: "Stepping Out of the Schedule"

Lynn reiterated Sheryl's comment in mentioning: "the calmer you are, it tends to bring the room down." Lynn had been at the institution-based center for a little over a year when I spoke with her. Of all the caregivers, she was the most recent graduate from an ECEC program. In her work setting, she was the only one (apart from the supervisor) with an under-three certificate. Lynn had also done the first level of RIE training and was very impressed with Magda Gerber (1979) and her ideas. However, in her job setting she had not yet been able to implement Gerber's philosophy as she might have wished.

Lynn reminded me of the importance of the team. She had been working with two very different caregivers, neither of whom have an infant-toddler certificate. As a staff, they have had little time to meet and discuss their beliefs and the program's philosophy. This has been challenging for Lynn, as she is enthusiastic about her work with babies and feels a commitment to doing an excellent job. As a new worker in the field, she has wanted to connect with others who share her enthusiasm: "Sometimes I just want to scream, because nobody seems to know where I'm coming from." Despite her alienation she worked hard to hold onto her beliefs and to work with the babies in a manner that was congruent with them. Not finding connections at work, Lynn turned to the local professional association, but was frustrated by its focus on preschool children. She wanted to meet "other infant-toddler caregivers working in the area I am working in now, to connect," and felt the frustrations of this work while seeking a forum to "find out how they cope and things like that."

In her setting, routines and policies have become directives for the work. This has created frustration:

> We have a case where the dad is going to school and the mom is working. So who comes when the child is sick? Do you miss school or do you take the time off work? And in most cases it is the parent who is attending school and then they get behind in their classes and they get frustrated with the doctors and staff, but what can we do? We have policies and they have to be met for the safety of all the children and the staff can't afford to be sick. It's frustrating, but that is part of the job.

Lynn knows caregivers need to have "the flexibility of stepping out of the schedule in order to calm things down" but in the setting where she works, it is difficult to do.

Mel: Just Beginning

Mel had been working at the school-based infant program for about a month when we talked. Previously, she had worked for seven years in a day care center with three-to-five-year-olds, but this was her first job in an infant program. As had Mary, she learned to take care of herself: "eat right and well, sleep well, keep fit, it's really a lot. You don't think of it being difficult, either, but it is." She acknowledged that it is a big change working with the infants and toddlers, "a big change." She also stated, "You have to be really flexible and you have to really be good at reading what's going on, really good at observing where they're at and what they need."

Mel eases into the job by using her powers of observation: "I sit back and watch and I wait for them to feel okay, wait for them to be familiar with me." She enjoyed watching the children: "I like watching them figure things out. That's what I like to watch. I like all sorts of stuff. It's how they interact with each other, how they build little friendships with each other. I like watching them interact, I think it's great."

Mel used observation to gain understanding of the children and to discover how the center operated. She commented, "You get that [understanding] through observing, to see how they work as a team and how to fit into the team." Mel watched her co-workers carefully to be able to participate in a helpful, attuned manner. In taking the time to observe the flow of the day, rather than immediately rushing in, Mel felt the acceptance of her co-workers.

Caring for babies requires a multitude of skills. Each caregiver had stories to tell that illustrated her individual approach, her style of caregiving. Through the narratives of these women, different facets of the infant-toddler caregiving practice are revealed. The caregivers must hold in their minds and their hearts several relationships, striving for an uneasy balance. Juggling these relationships creates tensions, as each demands varying levels of attention at different times or at the same time. Caregivers had reflected on these places of difficulty and tension and struggled to find possible solutions to the balancing act.

Chapter 8

Places of Difficulty

Three years old, Sam had arrived early that morning and after lunch it was clear he was ready for a nap. He was rubbing his eyes and slowing down. But once he was on his cot he squirmed and wiggled. While the others had quickly fallen asleep, he seemed to be fighting sleep; in fact, he was actually holding his eyelids open. I sat beside him and patted his back, but he seemed unable to relax, despite being tired. This was not his usual pattern. Finally, I picked him up, wrapped him in his blanket and held him like a baby. "Sam, it is okay to shut your eyes. I am right here. If you see anything scary when your eyes are shut, just open them and I will be here." I said this several times and he finally gave a shudder and a sigh and closed his eyes.

Later, having a cup of tea, I mentioned Sam's difficulty falling asleep to the social worker who visited the families in our program. Jokingly, I said to her, "If I didn't know better I would think his mother had taken him to see *The Exorcist*!"

"She did," replied the social worker. " It was what they did to celebrate his third birthday."

I was shocked and saddened. I had carefully avoided the movie myself, hating movies that scared and frightened.

As the caregivers spoke about the necessary balancing that multiple levels of relationship require, I had my own memories of the tensions embedded in the work. As Hector clung to the table leg while his mother screamed and pulled at him, I remember having a sense of his anxiety, as well as what seemed to be his mother's anxiety, the other children's anxiety, and my own anxiety. The tension of that moment seemed resolved when they left the room, but on a closer look, it remained with me. I had an awareness of the quality of relationship between Hector and his mother, and I needed to maintain relationships with both. The maintenance of individuality within a relationship is critical and creates tension. While being in relationship, there is always a risk of loss of self, of empathizing so closely that one loses perspective and a sense of self. Caring for another also means being vulnerable to grief at the loss of that person, of that relationship. Psychologist Robert Kegan (1982) wrote, "we can never protect ourselves from the risks of caring. In running these risks we preserve the connections between us. We enhance the life we share, or perhaps better put, we enhance the life that shares us" (p. 20).

The caregivers spoke of a variety of griefs that may appear small, but these daily small sorrows come from being attached to children and families. When caring for very small children and becoming attached to them, one does so with an awareness of their future departure. Saying good-bye to children as they move to another situation means the caregivers experiencing a loss—an anticipated loss—but a loss nevertheless. Caregivers also grieve the circumstances in which some babies live, for example, the poverty or the chaotic family situations that the babies live within. Were caregivers to ignore these realities of separation and loss or deny the reality of the lives of some children, they would be in danger of distancing themselves from the children in their care.

Grief

Maintaining their own separateness within a web of relationships proved challenging at times for the caregivers. Maintaining her own values while accepting parents' values could stretch a caregiver's empathy. Dawn has decided she has "an ear [for parents], to support and not judge." Judgment can maintain one's separateness, but it interferes with relationship.

Lynn seemed to feel torn trying to respond appropriately to each of the eleven children in her group. She had little time or patience for the parents, and her judgments of the parents appeared to create tension for her. She became frustrated when faced with a sick child and parents who keep sending the child into the center, saying, "Something that most of us at work get really frustrated about is when children are sick. You've called and talked to the parents to come pick them up and then the next day they are back again and you are thinking, why? You choose to have your children, you choose to raise your children, but sometimes it seems that the work is more important and they can't take that time to nurse their child back to health."

Her frustration was understandable. A sick child needs extra attention, and parents working in jobs with little room for sick time often are caught between their child and the job. Part of the problem is a system that does not give parents sufficient options and does not seem to value the work that caregivers do. Mary was able to encompass both points of view here and felt the difficulty of each. Her sympathies were with the child, yet she also understood the parental dilemma:

> Sometimes they would send their children in and I don't think they were healthy enough to be here. The child will need one-on-one and will be upset and you can tell they are obviously not feeling well. I'll phone the parent and if the baby doesn't have a temperature they need a few symptoms first. Then they will say, well, you know, I can't leave work, but, you know, if they have a temperature I'll come and get them. We can't force a temperature, but I know the child shouldn't be here. Sometimes, I wonder if they have been given Tylenol at home and things like that. And that is not okay, the tough part is you feel bad for the child and you know the parent is needing to be at work and they have their own pressures.

Caregivers must constantly address the conflicting feelings that arise from the commitment and caring they feel for the child, yet these feelings must be addressed so that their impact in other relationships is minimized. Judgments must be reframed so that both parent and child are encompassed in understanding. Caregivers spoke of learning from these places of uneasiness. Jade admitted, "I don't even like to say good-bye. I would rather not go to work. I thought, yes, this is something I need to work on." Of her education for under-threes, Dawn said:

> I didn't learn any of the stuff I'm learning now. You learn all
> the lingo and all the developmental stuff, but you don't learn
> the attachment, the caring, the love, the emotional connections,
> the relationship building. You don't learn any of that stuff. So
> you have to learn that stuff as you go. There is so much that
> you don't learn, so I'm really glad I did it the way I did it.
> Because I learned a lot through the moms and the babies I work
> with. I really feel like I didn't learn the most important stuff
> about how to work with the families, how to love them. It is all
> textbook stuff. I think you have to learn a lot when you are
> working with infants and children through modeling and
> watching and seeing. And working with other people. I've
> gotten a lot from the staff that I've worked with, so much. That
> is the biggest thing, the emotional side of it.

Saying good-bye is hard; struggling with the emotions of the
job took active engagement. Dawn acknowledged her feelings and
was open to learning about herself. Turning away from the self-
awareness that emotions offer could be a temptation in order to
simplify the process of caregiving, but none of these caregivers
chose that path. Perhaps this is the path chosen by the caregivers
described so poignantly in Leavitt's (1994) work. About saying
good-bye to some of the children in her care, Dawn said:

> I'm always bawling. I'm the one in the center who is always
> crying. That's just the way it is. I think because of the person I
> am, I really, really care. It's hard. It's really hard. I mean some
> are harder than others. You know, because, you know,...you
> have not your favorites, but you have children whom you are
> really connected with. And this year I actually have three
> whom I have been with for two years. It is the first group that
> I have had all of them—being with them and working with
> them all the time. It's going to be a hard year, because the
> moms are already talking about it. So they are feeling it too,
> which is incredible.

Parents also feel a loss, as does the child, when they move on.
Being aware of this loss and being able to discuss it with parents,
caregivers can understand and appreciate their own and each
other's feelings. The child can learn from the adults about ways to
negotiate these emotionally difficult times. Jade said it is important to feel the sadness of saying good-bye, because "it actually

hurts more to shut it down, because it is incomplete, it is unre-solved." To leave the emotions and connections unacknowledged had the potential to do more harm than good. Mary spoke about how painful it was to turn from saying good-bye to a baby who had been in her care, and to welcome a new baby immediately: "And then, you know, you may have a new baby the next day and it is like, 'I don't want my new baby yet, I want my old one back.' This one you don't know yet. It's tough, you've got to put them in the old baby's bed and it is very hard. Often the next day it happens."

It might be important to acknowledge the feelings of loss and sadness, but there is no time to grieve, given the practical realities of having to fill the empty space. Acknowledging the emotion and facing it takes not only time, but self-awareness. Faced with the sadness of saying good-bye, a caregiver may be tempted to shut down her emotions. Rachel needed to look closely at herself and her own background to understand her responses to closure and to saying good bye to families in her care. Unlike Dawn, the catalyst for Rachel's introspection had been a return to school where she was working on a BA in Child and Youth Care.

> I get really attached to the baby and really attached to the par-ents. And actually it is interesting, because right now in my class we are doing a lot of counseling [work, some of it] about closure. I never really thought about closure for myself. About how do I close. Like how do I say good-bye to infants and how do I separate. One good thing about where I work is that we often see the children for a very long time because they move from our center to the toddler center to the three-to-five center. So there is a good chance their children could stay in the center for five years, technically. So we have that ability to see them move through. But how do I deal with it? Well, you know, it's interesting, I never would have been able to articulate this until I had to [for her class]. I just ignore that it is even happening. And I was never even aware that it was even hap-pening. I'm the kind of person who would leave a party without saying good-bye. And I never realized I did that. But that's how I deal with it. but now I'm aware of it and I'm thinking, "Oh, my goodness, that's how I deal with it!" So now I think, let's go to a different place with this now. I'm ready to move to a differ-ent place with it. Really experience it. For me, I think it was about that loss of relationship.

Allowing herself to experience the loss of her relationship with a child deepened her practice and connected her to the loss the child was experiencing. Staying emotionally present to the tensions created by the losses kept the caregiver involved in her work.

Engaging with the emotions and difficulties that arose in their work required reflection and understanding of one's self and others. All of the caregivers thought about their work carefully. Sheryl said, "You go home, at least I do, you think about what happened that day and the things weren't quite the way you would want them to be. Because you want to provide the best care that you can. You are always thinking about other ways you could have done it. You continue to think. I don't think anyone could be perfect at a job or perfect in what they do, so you always have to be improving yourself."

Naming the emotions they struggled with, the losses they were experiencing and "looking at it from all angles," caregivers grew and learned about themselves and their practice, both within and through relationships. Benner and Wrubel (1989) suggest that "the person who learns to 'manage' (ward off, distance) emotions effectively eliminates the guidance and direction provided by those emotions" (p. 60). Sheryl found the theory different from practice, and she relied more on her hands-on experience to find strategies for coping with her practice:

> I found at university there was so much theory, so much theory. What was real was when you got into your practicum. That is when you learned the most. Because what you see on paper and what you actually do are maybe two different things. I know at university you do these theories; you have to know these differences and you know this theory and who did it and their principles and then they say, "Which one are you? Are you a behaviorist? Or are you a—?" It is like, I can't choose, you just pick what works for you and that's what you go for.

Wien (1995) said, "At the points of conflict lie the routes to change" (p. 131). Places of sadness, places of discomfort, can encourage reflection and discussion. At these points if caregivers can stop to look within and find "what works for them," they can bring an understanding to issues of separation, such as saying good-bye to a child to whom they feel close. Some centers have made space or time for reflection, for the articulation of and discussion of difficulties. Paying attention to these uncomfortable feelings can teach us, and by bringing this discussion more clearly into our practice we honor the caregiving process.

Tensions

F. Scott Fitzgerald (1963) said in his short story "The Crack-Up", that "the test of a first-rate intelligence is the ability to hold two opposing ideas in the mind at the same time and still retain the ability to function" (p. 405). Balancing relationships and the differing points of view of parents, staff, and one's self is not easy. Holding the tensions, balancing competing pulls in one's mind, is demanding work. Dawn acknowledged, "It is really hard to balance three children, really hard. I mean, you have them when they are sick and staff are away and you want to meet all of their needs." Lynn makes a similar statement, "So you are not always sure. You can only take one child at a time. That can be frustrating too." Sheryl commented, "I want to be able to meet all the needs, but that's not always possible, so you just do your best for one child, and then the next one, and the next one. And try to give each child what they need at the time, and it's hard sometimes."

Being stretched between the demands of three babies is difficult, but there are other pulls as well. Parents have their own beliefs and methods of handling their babies that can add another tension to the work. As Mary said of some of the babies she cares for, "Some babies are used to being propped up [in a sitting position] and we don't do that here. We don't prop them up if they're not sitting up on their own. That's tough. What we do is we try and find a balance. Of course, they don't want to lie down, because that's not what they get at home, so that's very hard. You can't leave them sitting, because it is not safe, they'll fall over. So that's very hard. There is a lot to deal with."

Caught between her desire to put babies in positions they can move in and out of themselves and the need to respect what is done at home, Mary tried to negotiate a compromise, to "find a balance," for the baby, the center, and the parents. The challenge is to not become immobilized by the tension of being in-between or by being pulled in different directions. This hard work requires constant attention and thought and an ability to find compromise. Sheryl said, "I stay calm by knowing that I'm doing the best I can. When I am feeding a baby, sometimes I just move close to another baby that's having a hard time, and say I've got so-and-so in my arms right now, but you're next! Just to convey that when I'm done with this child, the next one's coming up and then I'll look after you. I know you are hungry or maybe kind of verbalize what they might be needing at the time."

Sheryl acknowledges the anxiety of two babies needing her at the same time. She tries to stay calm and focus on what she is doing at the moment. Another strategy was to ask for help; Dawn felt that co-workers can absorb some of the tension for you. She said, "And, you know, personally, I'll speak for myself, but we all have those days when we are really tired and you say, 'Okay, I don't want you to scream at me any more.' That is when you say, 'Can someone come and deal with this child? I just can't cope anymore.' That is hard. I struggle with that, even though I love this and I care, I still have those moments when, 'Please take this child from me, because I can't handle it right now.' So that's my personal struggle."

Having the energy to deal with an unhappy baby when one's own resources are low can be challenging, A caregiver can be disappointed in herself that she is unable to deal with the crying or needs to ask for help, but knowing when to ask for support and calling on co-workers is one strategy for coping and maintaining balance when tensions mount.

At times caregivers were overwhelmed with decisions to be made and found that working in a team could spread out such decisions. The decisions and responsibilities are shared and thus lightened. Teamwork is not simple and when it is missing it creates yet another tension or stress for caregivers. Working cooperatively requires thought, trust, communication, and a willingness to give and get help.

In an attempt to streamline the work, and to simplify the decisions and tensions of the work, some programs try to put caregiving on a schedule. Working to a predetermined schedule does not often support *responsive* caregiving. Being on "diapers at ten" means changing twelve babies in a row, rather than a particular baby being changed within the context of personal relationship. Lynn, who worked in such a scheduled setting, said, "What we do is—the first person who arrives in the morning will do the morning set of diapers. The person who is in second will do the lunch bulk." This approach to caregiving reflects a mechanistic perspective. Caregiving is a task to be done rather than an engagement with individual babies in unique contexts. It robs babies of their individuality and caregivers of their agency.

Despite the attempts of the center to streamline and simplify the caregiving routines, Lynn did not feel that she could count on her co-workers as, for example, Dawn could. Lynn felt it was due to the other staff's lack of the necessary training: "I've never worked in a center where I haven't been surrounded by other infant-toddler workers. So it makes a huge difference." This might have been the reason. But the set routine also took away staff choice about how routines would be handled; the caregivers are subject to the schedule rather than in control of the schedule. An effective level of trust was absent among the caregivers in Lynn's center and she was uncertain what she could expect from the others. She said, "Well, you are not always sure. Because sometimes I'll think so-and-so is quite tired and you'd like to think that they will be the next one to go to bed and you come back [from lunch] and they haven't even gone in [to the nap room] yet. And you think, 'Well, why not?'"

These tensions can be too much to balance. Because she did not experience a collaborative process with her co-workers, the decisions were too much at times. Lynn sometimes seemed to feel overwhelmed with the different tensions and pulls on her attention, with no process to balance these competing tugs. "It is not written in the book and I don't know if I heard any of my instructors say how physically exhausting and how many decisions are made in a day. Constant decisions over the smallest of things and throughout the day, so many. You know, do I put this guy down for a nap now or later? Or do I send him out in the fresh air? And it is not one child, it is eleven children." The situation in which she worked gave Lynn and her co-workers little time to focus, to find the "rhythm of the dance," or to help each other.

Sheryl had also experienced disagreement with co-workers. She had experience in a previous work situation where she questioned

the philosophy of the center and the practice; the situation produced a great deal of tension for her:

> I worked in one center where they believed in self-calming.
> It's like they would say, "Let them cry." But, you know, when
> they reach that point where it's like, they're not even crying
> because they are trying to self-calm, they're crying because
> they just want someone to pick them up. They just want to
> interact with somebody, to be touched. And that was really
> hard for me, because they believed in the self-calming thing.
> But okay it's not working for that child, that child needs to be,
> or I think, it needs to be picked up. Maybe that's what they
> need. That's hard for me. You have to know what you want
> and how you want to work with the children. Because if you
> work in a center with a philosophy that you don't quite
> believe in or you don't believe in everything in the philoso-
> phy, it's too hard to work there because it's going against what
> you believe.

Finding a way to balance the tensions helps to diminish them.
When tensions are in balance they cease to claim you. When all is
working well and in balance, it is, as Dawn says, a "little dance
knowing that it is going to be okay." Caregivers found it challenging to prioritize the calls for their attention if they were unable to
count on a co-worker and needed to know they could depend on
co-workers as necessary. At times, a caregiver would use the
strengths of another staff member to resolve an issue with a family
or a child. Dawn said, "So it is about some issues you can't take on;
it is about passing it on to someone else, using your other team
members or Hetty [the supervisor]."

What Was Not Said

Participant caregivers spoke deeply of their work, its difficulties
and its rewards, its lessons and frustrations. Our discussions cov-
ered many of the issues that faced them in building and maintaining relationships, handling the tensions inherent in those
relationships, and in developing necessary relational skills. There
were also words left unspoken, subjects the women found difficult
to articulate, and areas of omission and opaqueness.

Complex Feelings

While reflective and open to discussing their work, these care-givers also found places in their practice that were difficult to address. In each discussion there were moments where one said something like, "It's hard to put in words," "I just can't get it out," "I feel I'm being murky right now," "I don't know what I'm trying to say." Most of these comments were made when trying to describe the complexity of feelings with which they were dealing. Saying good-bye to a child, for example, was painful when the child had been with a caregiver for a long while. The caregiver was aware that it was time for the child to move on, yet experienced sadness at the emptiness left by the child's departure; pleasure at the child's growing up was tinged with the sadness of loss. Caregivers were not used to acknowledging and focusing on these feelings. More accustomed to helping children with their feelings, supporting children's articulation of their anger or frustration, these women did not always have time for their own feelings.

There was little mention of anger as an emotion. Frustration with situations, difficult parents and crying babies were mentioned; frustration can certainly transform into anger, but anger was not a predominant feeling. Lynn was the closest to anger; it was directed at the situation in which she was working. Focused on explaining and communicating their feelings for their work, anger was not a dominant emotion. Perhaps if I had been asking more closely about how they felt about their status as child care workers I might have uncovered angry feelings. In fact, when I asked about this later, one caregiver got quite irate discussing with me the poor wages of caregivers.

Child Development

Although most ECEC programs teach the principles of caring for young children through a developmental lens, the caregivers did not often mention child development principles in our conversations. Their focus was primarily on the relationships they were building and maintaining. Rachel, who was currently in school, did mention child development theories and focused on attachment as the theory of most interest to her. Yet even Rachel stated that of greatest importance to her is "the real key relationship you have with them [the babies], the humourous relationship you have with them, when you can stay with them and work through that [relationship] with them, its always such a nice feeling for me."

She questioned some of the theories she was studying. "The other day I was reading about Erikson and his whole developmental thing about independence and autonomy. You should be pushing these infants and toddlers to go for that. But, in reality, we live in a very interdependent life, I think." Her practice had sensitized her to the dependence and interdependence of children, of all of us.

Because a relationship goes both ways, self-knowledge is as important as knowledge of the babies' personalities and developmental levels. Within relationship, both personal and developmental knowledge and skills are learned and tested and observation is an important skill. Sheryl says ["I gather things as I go;] gather methods, gather ideas as I go. I think that is how I have done it."

Intuition

Intuition was noted by caregivers, but once noted it seemed to escape precise understanding and description. Jade said, "I think intuition is a big part of it. I wasn't as tuned into my intuition then as I am now, or didn't believe in it as much. I don't think it's mind; I think the mind almost comes after." Others alluded to this type of knowing, which is neither linear nor necessarily rational. Mel says, "It's kind of a sense of everything that's going on around you, I think. Just knowing what's going on everywhere and where people are at and who might need something, and you have a sense."

I understood what they were trying to say regarding "intuition." Those years ago when Sam was having trouble going to sleep at nap time. I felt certain he was tired, very tired. I knew his "tired signals," as I knew those of the others in my small group of six two-year-olds. I cannot wholly articulate how I knew how to respond to Sam. With hindsight I might attempt to explain myself, but I am uncertain to this day what was actually at work. Vivian

Paley (1979) tells a similar story in her book *White Teacher*, about how the correct soothing words came to her as she spoke with a young brown girl in her class at the beginning of Paley's teaching career. Responding to the child's wish to look like the blond, pink-cheeked girl in a storybook, Paley said, "'Michelle, I know how you feel. When I was little I also would have liked to look like this little girl. She doesn't look like anyone in my family, so I couldn't have looked like her. Sometimes, I wish I had smooth, brown skin like yours. Then I could always be dark and pretty.' Michelle looked down at her skin. So did everyone else. I don't know what she was thinking. but I knew the feelings I had expressed were true, though I did not know it until I spoke" (p. 13).

Jade said, "I can probably tap into my intuition based on accumulated experience more than I could have at one time. Without a thought process, I could probably have been in a situation before and it comes out and I'll go with it." Intuition, the knowledge of when to rock and cuddle, or when to put a feeling or thought into words, may come with practice or may come into play from a nonverbal, noncognitive dimension. Benner and Wrubel (1989) would call this intuitive knowledge the knowledge of an expert practitioner. They say of the practice of expert nurses: "we cannot generalize by isolating effective actions and transferring the same interventions to another situation" (p. 4). These intuitive acts may contribute to the magic of caregiving.

Societal Silence

There is a silence surrounding the work of child care within society, and a seeming lack of interest and understanding regarding the job and all it entails. Despite society's professed honoring of young children, there is a significant inadequacy of support for families and their young children. Absence of regard is evidenced in the wages and status given to the work connected with babies. Doherty (1999b) observes, "There is no Canada-wide consensus about the goals for child care... there is no society-wide perspective on the characteristics of quality child care" (p. 70). Caregivers articulated their awareness of the powerful silence that they observed in the larger society. Sheryl said, "Because you tell people you are a daycare worker and they don't say it, but they think, 'Oh, just daycare.'" Lynn lamented, "We have such a responsibility and I think that is so overlooked." Mary said, "The average person who walks in and has a look, they're thinking, 'Well, how nice to just sit and play with babies all day. How nice.' They have no idea."

As Doherty et al. in the *You Bet I Care!* study (2000) reported, "the perception of not being valued or respected contributes to poor staff morale and turnover, and may impede recruitment of new workers into the field" (p. 179). Beach et al. (2004) concur that government policy does not reflect the "increasing aware- ness of the importance of early childhood development" (p. 7). The common perception is that it is not difficult and not demanding to look after babies. Previously, babies most often have been looked after at home or with relatives. In a sense, babies have been relegated to the private world of the family. In our society, both homemaking and raising and caring for the family have themselves been undervalued. Ways of nurturing and interacting with young children have been left out of the main- stream discussion. As Grumet (1988) says, "other people's chil- dren are abstract" (p. 173). For our own children we seek caregivers who offer quality caregiving, responsiveness, and who see the children as individuals. Several years ago I met with the supervisor of a university student working with our program. I offered to show him the baby program. He waved aside my offer with, "When you've seen one baby, you've seen them all." I hope his comment was meant as a joke but, in a deep way, I knew that it wasn't.

The women in this study have powerful skills, and they delib- erately and carefully reflect on their work. Society's assumptions that their work is easy, undemanding, or simple devalues and diminishes the knowledge and expertise caregivers bring to their job. While they infrequently mentioned this invisibility directly, each one acknowledged some difficulty with the dismissal of the value of their work. Rachel said, "Many people often feel lost when they work with infants. Like their identity as a worker is lost. I guess for me, when people talk about that, I always think, well, do they not see the value of what the infant is doing? Maybe they feel they are not doing anything valuable because they can't see the value of the infant? Because they are not acting, they are not doing?"

As well, distressing comments made by parents, perhaps intended as compliments, are noted. Mary said, "I have parents come and say, 'Well, you have a good day.' And it could be really loud in the room and crying and screaming. 'I don't know how you do it. I could never do your job.' I don't think people really understand how demanding it is." While a remark such as this appears empathetic and sometimes it is, it is often heard as dismissive. No one asks how the caregivers do the job, much less stops and listens to the answer.

Dismissal and lack of recognition create invisibility. The complexity and intricacy of the job is not acknowledged widely in society, as evidenced by the fact that in New Brunswick, the Northwest Territories, and the Yukon no training is even required to look after children (Childcare Resource and Research Unit, 2000). The caregivers in this study were aware of the difficulties and complex issues to be balanced and negotiated, but they are aware that their work remains largely unseen. "The debate about whether child care is primarily a private or public responsibility continues" (Beach et al., 2004, p. 5). Not only is the job invisible to the public, but the caregivers are also part of children's lives at a time when memory is nonverbal. Parents will remember the caregivers, and while the children may remember the connection on a nonverbal level, it is likely to be an unconscious remembering. Thus the invisibility happens on many levels.

Though some participants mentioned the lack of public recognition, they did not mention the low wages and minimal benefits for caregivers. This is an acknowledged problem in the field (Beach, Bertrand, and Cleveland, 1998;   Beach et al., 2004 Doherty et al., 2000). Perhaps it was not mentioned because I did not specifically ask about wages and benefits, but we were conversing widely and no one raised the topic. It should also be pointed out that the centers in which these caregivers worked paid wages that were, on the whole, better than the average wage for an early childcare worker. Each center was well established and also had its own cachet for which it was known and respected. The college-based program had the prestige of the college behind it. The work-site center was seen as a proponent of the RIE method and had been started by a woman well respected in the field; this program also had a board of parents who worked hard to ensure as best they could good wages and benefits for caregivers. The school-based program worked closely with the school and counselors to support the students/mothers; the day care felt part of a dynamic culture working to make a difference in the young women's lives. The institution-based program was an old, established program, well known in the community.

When I went back to the caregivers to address the themes emerging from our discussions, I asked each woman about these areas of silence. Their reactions were similar to what I have just described. Several suggested that the silence about wages and status meant that people liked their jobs enough to make wages and status a non-issue. Only one person addressing wages and benefits with me spoke of deploring the situation of childcare workers.

Three of the four centers also had an internal culture that validated the work of their caregivers. At the work-site center, the parents worked hard to raise extra money to keep wages up and child-adult ratios low. The school-based program had a countercultural self-image, believing that they were different from the mainstream and seeing their success reflected in the eventual success of the young women in the program. This program had also managed to negotiate relatively good salaries and had such perks as school professional days and holidays. The college-based program was a large center with the unionized staff having pride about the quality of their program, which was a consistent practicum site for the college's early childhood education program. Within particular programs and centers, internal beliefs, stories, and cultures may have a bolstering effect against the prevailing metanarrative that devalues the work of caregivers.

Conclusion

The caregivers' relationships with the babies in their care took balancing, as did maintaining the relationships with parents, coworkers, and one's self. Building and maintaining relationships took empathy, trust, and reflection. Inevitably there were tensions that disturbed the delicate balance of relationship. Juggling three babies, understanding a parent's concerns, negotiating time with co-workers, saying good-bye to a baby you have cared for over the year, all took a considerable amount of a caregiver's time and energy. Understanding those tensions and paying attention to the relational aspects of the work helped caregivers negotiate their place in the web.

Caregivers may feel that their work was invisible and unrecognized, but all realized their involvement in the lives of children was important and fulfilling, filling both a societal need and their own personal needs for being engaged in valuable work. I believe it is through their reflection and thoughtfulness that these caregivers have come to situated beliefs that sustain good practice. When their work context supported their beliefs, their potential for excellent practice was maximized. They believe, as Mary Catherine Bateson (2000), an anthropologist interested in children, said: "Human infants survive only if they receive loving care. The memory of that care remains as a basis for the ability to give and receive care, while trauma in childhood may produce adults with limited abilities not only to give and receive love but also to learn" (p. 187).

Chapter 9

Supportive Contexts

During my time at the infant care unit I had in my group a girl named Lakshmi. She was a small, quiet girl. She had been coming regularly for seven months or more when she began to experience difficulty saying good-bye to her mother. She clung to her and screamed and screamed. I tried a number of things to make it easier for her in the mornings. Finally, I asked Dr. Lilleskov for suggestions. He listened carefully. After discussing the situation we came up with a strategy. I was ready each morning with a small doll house and three small figures.

When Lakshmi arrived I called her over and showed her the *lakshmi doll*, the *mommy doll*, and the *enid doll*. Each morning we had the *lakshmi doll* say good bye to the *mommy doll* and hello to the *enid doll* and then we would remember together that the *mommy doll* would come again in the evening and Lakshmi would say hello to her and good-bye to the *enid doll*.

Lakshmi soon used this ritual to make the transition to daycare. One morning she turned the *lakshmi doll* to face away from the *mommy doll* when we came to the part of the ritual where the *mommy doll* came to pick her up.

Later, debriefing this change with Dr. Lilleskov, who served an advisory role in the program, he suggested that I articulate what Lakshmi might be feeling about being left by mother in the morning. The next day I said that the *lakshmi doll* was feeling mad at the *mommy doll* for leaving her when Lakshmi turned the *lakshmi doll* to face away

137

from the *mommy doll*. She laughed and laughed. She repeated the action, turning the figure away from the mother figure and I repeated what I had said. Again she laughed and laughed. That was the last day she was interested in our morning ritual and it was the last day she had real difficulty in the morning.

To offer Lakshmi support I needed some myself. That support was more than the advice and debriefing offered by Dr. Lilleskov; the supervisor knew of our plan and scheduled an extra staff person to be in the room, allowing me to focus solely on Lakshmi. It was for a limited time and it made a difference.

Visiting the centers of the participants in my study, I observed how influential the setting is to the caregivers' ability to focus on her job; each setting was different from every other setting. A picture emerged of how the setting affected practice. Doherty (1999a) refers to the context as the "organizational climate," and says, "it has been described as the distinct atmosphere or personality that permeates a child care program, whether it be warm, supportive and enthusiastic or harsh, mistrustful and tense" (p. 23). The atmosphere permeates all levels from the children's program to the administration's attitude to the staff. All levels are interconnected. Embedded in their work sites, caregivers did not always seem aware of the impact the context had on their practice.

Context includes far more than physical surroundings. Caregivers may have some control over aspects of the physical setting. Depending on design, caregivers can moderate the setting to affect the tone within the space (e.g., lights can be regulated and surfaces can be softened or hardened). Yet control of the larger context can be elusive and the setting's locus of control can be difficult to determine. The word *context* means "a weaving together" (Fowler and Fowler, 1964) and involves elements, such as administrative attitudes, scheduling, co-workers, weaving together to create the work situation. The manner in which the administrators regard the caregivers in their program, consult them about the planning, and organize their time affects the working context. One cannot always be conscious of the subtle messages one receives from a working situation. The women in this study did not have a complete awareness of the messages within their contexts, since they were embedded in them. As an outsider, I could identify particular elements in their situations that stood out for me as troublesome or helpful.

Physical Setting

Environment plays a crucial role in our lives. Our surroundings give us many messages on conscious and unconscious levels, as a given space can convey a message of safety and relaxation or of risk and tension. There are many factors that contribute to the messages we receive and each of us has a different way of reading and interpreting a space. We have differing tolerances for temperature, noise, and light and have differing needs for stimulation and calm.

I have seen babies become attached to physical context, to the environment that they see, hear, and feel. Some babies are particularly in tune with their physical surroundings. At one year old, Kate was such a child. One afternoon, the caregivers in her program decided to change the set-up to meet the needs of the growing infants in her cohort. Many of the children were asleep and the caregivers moved a shelf and some mats to allow the infants, who were beginning to walk, more space. When Kate awoke to a new environment she started to cry, much to the puzzlement of the caregivers. Eventually the caregivers figured out the problem and placed the shelves and mats in their original places. They later made changes gradually, moving the furniture when Kate was awake and watching.

Environments can be designed so that caregiving practice is easier. Changing diapers, feeding babies, soothing an upset toddler are all part of the process of caregiving; a well-organized changing area, a comfortable feeding spot, a cozy spot in which to sit, all can contribute to a feeling of competence and validation. The institution-based center had a diapering area down the hall and isolated from the rest of the program. They also had a routine of diapering all the babies at one time by one person. Not only did this contribute to a feeling of babies as part of a production line, but made changing diapers a distasteful task as caregivers were isolated for that time slot, changing twelve babies with no sense of being connected to the rest of the program. Other programs had the changing area nearby, within earshot, and caregivers changed a baby when the child needed it. The caregiver remained connected to the program.

In most of the settings I found thoughtful planning: comfortable chairs for feeding infants, bottles efficiently warmed, cozy spots on the floor that made it easy for staff to sit on the floor and focus on the babies and toddlers. The school-based program had even found another room to use when the toddlers' needs outgrew their room.

Co-workers

Working effectively with babies and their families meant working as a team with co-workers. "It can be very difficult if the staff are not getting along, you can feel it. We work so closely together that the communications line just has to stay open," acknowledged Mary. Pinpointing the need for experienced and educated colleagues, Sheryl, who had experience in several different infant centers, said, "This place is lucky, because their ratios are lower and there are less [fewer] children. They're not trying to skimp on money by trying to hire newer people from the field so they can pay them less. They are all high-quality caregivers. [Sometimes] you go to another center, [with] all these people just out of school and you have [only] one person that's experienced. That one person can't carry all the other new people."

Three of the four centers were determined to have experienced and qualified staff and to keep the ratio at one caregiver for three babies. The fact that these programs attempted to exceed the licensing standards and aim for quality care for children gave a message to both staff and parents that caregiving is important and valued work. In the fourth center, the caregiver said, "It's been challenging, because I've always worked in centers where they have gone beyond the standards of minimum requirements for infant-toddler needs. I've never worked in a center where I haven't been surrounded by other infant-toddler workers. So it makes a huge difference." Rachel acknowledged that she has had difficulties come up in the room when "you are dealing with staff who haven't necessarily worked with infants and they are at a really beginning stage and you are at a different stage."

With a ratio of one caregiver for four babies in the center where Lynn worked, with the exception of the supervisor, Lynn was the only under-three trained caregiver. When I was there, the woman relieving the caregivers at lunch was in the last year of her training to be an elementary school teacher. She had not been in the room before and did not know the names of the infants. With this lack of coherence among the caregivers, Lynn acknowledged that it would be good to have "more time to discuss things. You have programming time at staff meetings, but that is once a month. You can't wait for once a month if you have something that needs to be discussed now, especially if there are things that aren't being done and need to be done."

If staff are not experienced or knowledgeable about working with infants and toddlers, taking time to meet and organize would promote teamwork and learning on the job. Staff members need each other and they need time to talk. Dawn says that she deals with difficult issues by talking with "the staff, I do a lot of talking about it." Mary felt that staff worked to resolve disagreements—"so if disagreements came up or different issues came up I'm pretty sure they'd be talked about on a good level...they just seem so open to lots of things and ideas...." Not only could staff help each other by listening, but by listening with an openness that created trust and offered new perspectives.

Supervision

Though I did not ask directly about supervision, it became clear from comments caregivers offered at points in our discussions that a supervisor could be very helpful regarding practice and perspective. As well, supervisors support and assist when staff debrief, and supervisors are the liaisons between staff and administrative boards or funding bodies. As Jorde-Bloom (1988) noted, "facilitative and supportive administrators" help create a positive climate for child care workers. A good supervisor allows opportunities for staff to build relationships, helps them negotiate tensions they may discover within those relationships, and supports them in deepening their own self-knowledge. Deeply involved in their relationships, caregivers can benefit from the supervisor's perspective.

Support can come from an administrative environment that values the caregivers and from supervisors who speak up for their staff members, providing support and offering other perspectives on given situations. Mary mentions it is "just nice to know that she's [the supervisor is] there to back you up if you have any problems, things like that." Caregivers engaged in good practice, supported by their co-workers and supervisors and administrations, gather knowledge, experience, and wisdom that enhance their work. A supervisor can create an environment that supports and protects the caregiver in the uncertainty of dealing with the inevitable tensions of working within different relationships. She can protect her staff by having a relationship with them that is predictable, responsive, and sensitive. In a secure and nurturing environment caregivers can feel safe enough to take risks and extend themselves emotionally.

The supervisor can offer the debriefing and feedback that helps to provide perspective on work that can be intense and difficult. Everyone agreed that getting feedback was useful; Jade said, "it is just getting another perspective or just a reminder that you have done your best." This support can assist in the relationship-building necessary for good care. A supervisor needs to provide and model the caring and responsiveness with the staff that she wants the caregivers to bring to their relationships with babies and families, and as Mary says, "she is there to back you up if you have any problems." Like the babies, the caregivers need to know that someone supports them and has their interests at heart.

Working within relationship with staff, the supervisor cannot rely solely on a structure of rules and regulations to guide her, necessarily using the same skills that the staff use to build trust through empathy and thoughtfulness. She also has her own knowledge of children and families and her knowledge of working with emotional issues and tensions.

Institutional Context

Working in a center that values the training of its staff and supports the provision of good care validates the work of the women caring for children. A supportive context can also help to negate the larger societal perceptions that caring for young children is merely "custodial." The four centers my participants worked in run counter to a general trend of poor working conditions for early childhood caregivers (Beach et al., 2004). Not every staff can meet with the regularity of the school-based program, but some do find time. Mary said:

> We have a staff meeting every two weeks and we always make a point of discussing the children and families. We also have a daily communications book. We check it in the morning when we come in. People can write down important things that come up or how they're feeling. We check in with each other during the day, but we don't have a lot of time during the day for social chat. We're also on different shifts and schedules, so there's no real time where we can all sit down during the day, so we do need the communications book where we can keep on top of things. And you watch each other, you can tell if someone is getting a little stressed out, and maybe help out with that, help with a person's child.

It did seem to make a difference to the caregivers when staff had good training, when ratios were smaller than those set by regulations, when group size was small, and when staff met more regularly. This perception is affirmed by other research, including that of Sullivan, Bose, and Levesque (1999). Primary caregiving also made a positive difference: each of the three centers with lower ratios also used a primary caregiving system. The fourth center used primary caregiving in a somewhat inconsistent way. Lynn said, "We try to keep some consistency from home to daycare. If the parent needs to be contacted throughout the day, the primary caregiver would do that. We don't do it in the way that some centers do it. I'm not the only one that diapers my four children, I'm not the only one that will feed my four children."

In the other centers, the caregiver had three children whom they fed, diapered, and put to sleep. Focusing on the same three children over time allowed caregivers more meaningful relationships with both children and their parents. Lower ratios, staff meetings, and primary caregiving allowed staff more time to do thoughtful work. The fact that the administration backed this system validated their practice within the work setting.

Through primary caregiving, a caregiver can develop a deep relationship with the baby and, sometimes, with the parents. Working as part of a team, balancing relationships with children and families, and taking care of themselves is a complex balance. In order to simplify this complex web of connections, programs

sometimes try to confine babies and people into policies, schedules, and tasks. Changing a child becomes "diapers" and the day
becomes ruled by the routine.

This is a questionable solution, as the focus becomes the task
instead of the individual baby. The job can become one of paying
attention to the rules and discrete tasks, instead of engaging in a
reflective practice, such as when parents, taking time to enjoy their
child in a morning when they don't need to be at work early, are
turned away at the door because a program does not accept children after ten o'clock. Rules and schedules can simplify life, but if
they lead to mindless repetition of tasks, if tasks become an end in
themselves, then they interfere with a caregiver's focus and attention on what is actually developing within their relationships
(Langer, 1989). This focus promotes a mechanistic view of babies
as objects to be controlled and handled, resulting in a system
where caregivers are controllers keeping to a schedule and accomplishing a set of tasks.

Feeling valued, having time for reflection, and having support
to develop meaningful empathic relationships contributes to caregivers developing thoughtful practice; working to a schedule and
regulations contributes to the creation of a very different atmosphere. Observing in the fourth center, I found myself beginning to
see the children as a group or herd. The context had exerted a
strong influence on me. After being there, I wrote:

> November 10, 1999,
> The babies are outside crying and they want to come in.
> Three are allowed inside, but there are a couple more outside
> looking in. I feel they are managing numbers here and that the
> children are more like a herd. Perhaps it is not possible any
> other way? There is one child crying at the window. Why don't
> they pick him up? Now there are two children crying at the
> window. Could one come in with the caregiver fixing the
> lunches? Two faces pressed to the window. "He likes to be
> picked up and we can't do that right now," I am told.

Of the centers I observed, only at this institution-based program did the children not stand out as individuals. Perhaps this
reflected the fact that the children had simply become tasks with
which to deal. Lynn was calm and worked diligently to speak
gently to the children, and the other caregivers at the institution-

based center also were kind and worked hard, but the organizational context worked against them all. Their jobs were clearly focused on routines and getting tasks completed.

In an attempt to connect meaningfully with parents at the institution-based center, staff began to take photos and created a photo board. Lynn said:

> We started to take photos and put them on the bulletin board. We seemed to change the photos every second month. We take snapshots of their children during the day, doing different things and we'll put them up. If we get a double set of prints, the second ones go home with the parents. That's one thing we have started to do and the parents like it. We have a bulletin board of the families, the children, and their parents. It's just outside the door and you see the children pointing up to the picture of their mom and their faces just light up.

The staff paid for this from their own pockets although Lynn acknowledged that if one remembered to bring in the receipt, she could get reimbursed. The staff had initiated this idea and then enjoyed the reactions of parents and children, yet the administration had not responded enthusiastically to their efforts. An opportunity to acknowledge staff initiative and efforts went unrecognized.

From my observations and conversations with Lynn, the institution-based program employees demonstrated a lack of common vision. Lynn indicated that staff members did not share the same philosophy of infant-toddler care. The administration did not share a common vision with staff. Staff members tried to sporadically enhance and deepen their work with little support from administration. Not enough communication happened amongst or between staff members and there was little dialogue with administrative staff. Within a supportive context, staff can make meaning of the work they do and find an approach that supports their own development as unique human beings within a shared working situation. If staff lack the opportunity to debrief and understand the work's tensions and complexities, they may internalize the struggle, or simply give up. Administrative support and advocacy *could* create a counterculture to the dominant discourse that diminishes and ignores caring work. While wages can only be raised to a level realistic with the current funding situations, caregivers feel appreciated when they are aware that the administration is doing all it can to funnel resources to support them.

Parents on the board of the work-site center worked hard to fundraise to up staff salaries and to keep the ratio of 3:1. The college-based program was unionized, their wages were good, and they had an administrator who advocated for her staff with the college administrators. The school-based program was run by a society that valued the staff and tried to keep salaries up, while the supervisor worked to build in perks, such as staff having an "early day" if the number of children were down.

Time

From the interviews, a tension emerges in the way that time is conceptualized. The management of time is an issue: not having enough time to meet or enough time for reflection. Caregivers indicated that they need time to debrief, to think aloud, and to reflect with their co-workers. To build a relationship takes time to best understand the position and perspective of a family, a child, or a co-worker. The routines of the day must be organized.

The management of time was approached differently. Conceiving of time as linear and dividable into chunks seemed to simplify the day and give a sense of efficiency. Time conceived of as multidimensional, with an awareness of the baby's pace while varying the caregiver's pace to meet the situations, seemed more complicated and yet seemed to fit with the notion of being responsive and relational. On the surface, the latter concept seemed less clear, as Sheryl noted that no two days were the same. Wien (1995) has studied the issue of time extensively and suggests that, "teachers' work is conflicted, contradictory, muddied, and torn by myriad demands of a dynamic lived life in which each teacher must negotiate her way, shaping small moments as she is shaped by the very things she takes most for granted—especially conceptions of use of time" (p. 144). Caregivers' work seems to be no different.

A community, however small, develops strategies over time to deal with a variety of logistical problems. These strategies often become fixed, are usually unquestioned, and their usefulness may often become outgrown. As I listened to caregivers and observed in the centers, I noticed how I was influenced in whatever setting I found myself. Each context had physical factors that impacted me, as well as less tangible ones. As Langer (1989) writes, "The way we behave in any situation has a lot to do with the context" (p. 35). Part of the context is the temporal flow of the day. I concur with Wien (1995), who writes of the scripts that are set in place and are usually "inherited," not chosen, by teachers/caregivers where they work. Scripts, once inherited, are often accepted and not questioned.

Time was an intangible factor in each context. We are not always aware of time as an element we organize and control, letting ourselves be determined by schedules and routines instead of perceiving such routines as merely tools for possible order. The caregivers' situations either supported the need for time to reflect and to build relationships or did not acknowledge and honor this need.

Being in control of the schedule, the caregivers in the school-based program were comfortable with the unpredictability of each day. The schedule was loose enough to accommodate a baby's extraordinary needs one day yet have the assurance of a routine. Each day had the same sequence, but the routine bent and flexed according to children's needs. Children and adults need to be comfortable with knowing that lunch is coming at a similar time each day, but if everyone is hungry half an hour early one day, meeting that need makes the day easier.

Having control of the schedule, while creating more decisions for caregivers, validates their role and credits their ability to organize the day to suit the program. To be responsive to the children in their care they need the responsibility of organizing the day in response to the children's needs daily, as well as generally. They are the best judges of how best to meet the children's needs and their own needs that day, but caregivers may need to learn to treat time as a flexible aspect of the environment.

Education and Training

Accepting Shonkoff and Phillips's (2000) premise that "children grow and thrive in the context of close and dependable relationships that provide love and nurturance, security, responsive interaction, and encouragement for exploration" (p. 389), means paying attention to the caregivers' narratives of practice and honoring their perspectives. If relationship is the most important aspect of care, the reward and focus for caregivers, then it is crucial that aspects of the education for infant-toddler caregivers be reconsidered. The study of relationship dynamics, specific training in relationship skills, and practice in reflective thinking would be useful additions to the curriculum for infant and toddler caregivers.

The women in this study had chosen to be infant-toddler caregivers, taking the courses and doing the practicum, and all said they had learned from the job and from their experiences. Dawn stressed that in the ECEC program "you learn all the lingo and all the developmental stuff, but you don't learn the attachment, the caring, the love, the emotional connections, the relationship building. You don't learn that stuff." Others agreed with her. The "caring, the love, the emotional connections" are key elements in caring for babies, but where does one find a curriculum for care and love, and what would it look like?

While Rachel felt that her educational coursework had offered her a chance to reflect and renew her practice, she stressed what she learned from the relationships she built with babies and parents. In particular, she spoke of a university-level course that focused on understanding her own history of relationships as they impacted on her practice. Rachel said, "I think there is a certain amount of skills and technique that you use, but if you go back to the philosophy, respecting the person that you are and not being anyone else—it totally freed me." Learning to be yourself involves self-knowledge. These caregivers stress a knowledge that is more than ages and stages of child development, more than health, safety, and nutrition, though these are important areas of knowledge. These women worked with a trust in their abilities, in their team; they created trust in the relationships they built, using empathy to guide them in their practice. They practiced reflective thinking as a method of understanding their practice and themselves more deeply. While there is no easy answer for teaching these skills, it is important to begin the discussion of how these skills can be brought into the training of ECEC practitioners, most particularly infant-toddler educators. Certainly as instructors of ECEC we can model this approach with our students.

Conclusion

With support, caregivers can focus on the relationships they are developing. A working environment that is efficient, pleasant, and validating creates a background that facilitates good care. Struggling to reach a diaper or the disinfectant while changing a baby takes the focus from the child. Having a comfortable spot to feed or soothe an infant is essential to being effective.

The encouragement and strength of teammates and supervisor can make an enormous difference. The baby or toddler needs the security of a relationship with a caregiver in the day care, while the caregiver needs the security of her co-workers' support. The staff needs the validation of a board or administration. Being embedded in a system that values the work and the workers helps caregivers work thoughtfully and carefully.

Valuing the process of relationships within a program can focus the supervisor's efforts and the administrative direction of the program. Time for meeting to discuss ideas and to hear co-workers' perspectives was valued by caregivers in this and other studies. When Jorde-Bloom (1998) looked at the influential elements in a group of centers highly rated for their organizational climate, she noted that one element was "innovativeness," which meant diverse opinions were encouraged, problem solving was valued, and there was a willingness to be adaptive. This can only occur in an atmosphere of trust, where time is set aside for discussion. When adults are problem solvers, they encourage problem solving in children. When adults are aware of their own emotions and care for themselves, they encourage children to do the same. Another key element in Jorde-Bloom's study was "goal consensus": the staff shared a common vision. Jade said that "we do share a common philosophy," which made collaboration easier in her center.

Chapter 10

Conclusion

My interviews sensitized me to the depth of emotion quietly felt by caregivers of babies and toddlers. When I told the story of Hector and spoke of my understanding of the emotional work done by caregivers at an National Association for the Education of Young Children (NAEYC) conference, this understanding seemed to resonate with the group. Following the presentation, Teresa Cosgrove (personal commment) of Point Roberts, Washington wrote eloquently to me of her own experience.

> I left my job at a community college child care center this fall. I was the primary caregiver for a group of ten 18-to-36-month-old toddlers for nine months. During that time the children had two different teachers and three different assistants as well as turnover of about half the class each of the three semesters and additional caregivers if they stayed late in the day. The number of separations they had to endure and the feelings of confusion, abandonment, and anger that followed made me think carefully about how I wanted to say goodbye to them. One almost-three-year-old in particular showed me that she missed the caregivers who had left but wasn't sure that they missed her. Despite my determination to be more mindful about my departure, I had difficulty thinking about how to handle it because of my own feelings of guilt about leaving them and the anticipated pain of

saying good-bye. Three weeks before my departure I missed five days of work due to illness. When I returned, two children were very angry with me. They avoided eye contact, scowled at me from a distance, and went out of their way to ask complete strangers for help rather than ask me. Their behavior made me realize that I couldn't avoid thinking about saying good-bye much longer.

Two weeks before I planned to leave, I started talking about it, mostly when the children were a captive audience in the buggy on our daily walks. I told them that soon I wouldn't be able to come and play anymore. I said I would be moving to a new house and it was so far away that I wouldn't be able to drive to school anymore. One child asked what color my new house was. When I said that I didn't know yet, she suggested it should be pink. I emphasized that I would miss them and described missing as a kind of sadness. Like sadness, I said it would feel bad but that after a while it would feel better. I wasn't sure how much the children understood until later in the week. During a walk, a dog frightened a flock of geese that we visited regularly. Their flight was very noisy and dramatic and the children watched silently as they darkened the sky above us. Before we finished our walk we returned to see if the geese had come back yet. When I mentioned that they weren't back yet, an almost two-and-a-half-year-old started calling, "Geese, come back! We miss you geese. Come back!"

I started to step back in the classroom. I asked my new assistant (she started a month before I left) to take over most of the diapering so that she could build a closer relationship with the children more quickly. I encouraged her to spend more time in the rocking chair. It was very difficult for me to see her there with a child in her lap, looking at a book or just cuddling or rocking. I longed for that intimacy, but I wanted just as much for the children to feel that they could turn to her after I left.

During my final week there, my assistant took Polaroid pictures of me with each child for them to keep. I also wrote a card to each family explaining how hard it was for me to say good-bye, how much I valued the trust they placed in me, and how much I would miss their child. I mentioned something that I would miss about each child. Toward the end of the week, I brought in a gift that I thought the children would enjoy and that I felt would fill a gap in what the toddler room offered. I donated a baby doll, with a change of clothing and a variety of accessories for feeding and caring for it. I called the doll the "good-bye baby" when I introduced the children to her. I reminded the children that I wouldn't be coming to play any-more, but that the baby would be staying for them to play with. They asked me, "Is she your baby?" I said that she was but that I was giving her to them.

Although I felt satisfied with the way I prepared the chil-dren for my departure, it wasn't until I started to tell my story at your NAEYC presentation that I paid attention to how little I had done to acknowledge the depth of my grief at leaving them. I still miss them. A month after my departure, this is still a tearful story to write. I plan to send them a picture of myself in front of my new house with a letter. Although this feels like the right place to stop writing, it doesn't feel like the end of my story. Taking the time to write this much of it reminds me that a grieving process continues outside of mundane awareness and in a sort of alternate universe: the one where I cared deeply for individual children who each needed me in a different way and who each trusted me to care for them in a way that gave our relationship meaning as well as purpose.

The narratives of Dawn, Jade, Mel, Sheryl, Lynn, Rachel, and Mary spoke broadly to other caregivers in the field. The sto-ries they shared with me had spoken of feelings and thoughts that had triggered memories in other women involved in the complicated work of caring. By sharing our stories of caring, by listening to each other, we will better understand the world of the infant-toddler caregiver. Ryan, Oschner, and Genish (2001) state, caregivers are "involved in a complicated web of social relationships that create possibilities as well as constraints" (p. 55). Including their voices in the discourse concerning care for infants and toddlers mandates consideration of this work from another, broader perspective.

These women all know that their work is a good deal more than babysitting, and would agree with Pence and Benner (2000) that "there are no simple answers" (p. 152) in the business of caring for babies. Articulating the interwoven relational, emo-tional, and intellectual threads of caregiving is often difficult, as the practice of caring is often assumed rather than named. From the narratives of the caregivers the shape and substance of their practice emerges, as Smith (1987) would say, "the forms of thought and images" (p. 35) begin to appear.

While the caregivers in this study spoke of the richness and complexity they experienced in their practice generally, the shared perception among caregivers was that their work was not valued or noticed. In the recent study *You Bet I Care!*, Doherty et al. (2000) report that there is "a substantial increase in the extent to which teaching staff and directors feel that their work is not valued by the general public" (p. 179).

Articulating Practice

The public is unaware of the complexity of the caregivers' work. By clarifying and illuminating the practice of caring for young children, the work can be more clearly seen. As caregivers begin to deepen their understanding of practice, and realize its meaning and value for them, they will begin to speak more clearly to public misconceptions and to each other about their work.

When I worked with Hector at the infant care unit in New York City (see chapter 1), I was a new teacher with a new MA in Early Childhood Education. After a few months, a keen student from Bank Street College of Education came to do a practicum with me. As she was my first practicum student, I was tentative about how to help her. At the start of her practicum, she spent time simply observing. At the end of each day, she would ask me why I had done this or that, and at times I would feel irritated with her. I had done "it" because "it" worked, could she not see that? I began to realize that while I had created a world that worked for me and for the children, articulating the "what" and "why" was difficult. I needed to develop a framework for the process in which I was engaged; the director of the program encouraged me to begin to reflect on my experience.

Articulating one's practice can be a deeply personal process requiring close attention, mindfulness, and reflection; caregivers needed support for this process. Rachel, for example, returned to college to define her practice more clearly. The caregivers in the school-based program developed the habit of meeting regularly to discuss the program, their own practices, and their evolving directions. Mary, though working in the program where she had begun her career as a young woman fresh out of school, had grown into herself with the support of, and opportunities offered by, more experienced staff. Lynn sought support for her process of making meaning and gaining understanding through her work, but did not find it. Her particular workplace did not offer much opportunity for discussion or shared thoughts, and her local professional organization did not offer this support either. Each of the caregivers I spoke with had found or tried to find support and community for further exploration and articulation of their practice.

By articulating the practice of caring, the webs of connectedness, the reasons for not becoming "a robot," become clearer. By becoming more aware of what happens in the process of caring for babies and toddlers we can deepen and enrich our practice. Creating conversations about the issues of working in relationship with babies and their families will help infant-toddler caregivers develop a community of practitioners.

Relationship as Focus

When I started this journey of inquiry, I could not have articulated so clearly the centrality of relationships to work in this field. As a caregiver and an ECEC instructor, I have experienced the enormous intellectual, emotional, and spiritual demands of this field, and on a personal level, I knew the considerable interpersonal skills needed for this work. The narratives of these women provoke discussion and reflection, and indicate they are clearly not "robots" involved in a mechanistic process. Their practice is one of engagement with self, others, and the early childhood community.

Engagement for the caregiver means a commitment; it is a promise to spend the time, energy, reflection to stay sensitive to the babies and families in her care. It is a pledge to be responsive.

The caregivers I mentioned were all engaged in their practice and saw their relationship to their practice as dynamic, challenging, and worthy of reflection. But caregivers can choose to not engage (Leavitt, 1995); the choice is theirs. They may choose to disengage from developing close relationships with babies to avoid the uncertainty, ambiguity, and intensity inherent in building and maintaining connections. The tensions that are part of being fully engaged in practice and the challenge of relationships with babies and families may prove too much to take on. Marris (1993) says that "a society that best protects its members from grief and depression would organize its relationships so that they were as stable, predictable, understandable, and careful of attachments as is humanly possible" (p. 83).

By nature, relationships are complex, dynamic, and uncertain. As these women have described, relationship is an ongoing and developing process. Babies grow and change, families grow and adjust, while caregivers respond to these changes and make changes of their own. Jade said, "I just do the best with who I am and with who they are. It is quite a combination—parent, child, your other staff. There are so many factors." The web of relationships is not static; it moves, shifts, and changes shape.

Relationships are at the heart of the work and are what "keeps them in the job" (Doherty et al., 2000, p. 172). Doherty's respondents indicated that it was the "nature of the work" that was positive and this included "love from the children, a varied and stimulating job, and a people-oriented job" (p. xx). The Canadian Child Care Federation/Canadian Day Care Advocacy center's (1992) study of Canadian child care providers reported caregivers as being most satisfied with and liking those aspects of work that involved contact with children. Goelman and Pence (1987) noted that for licensed family day care providers, satisfaction was connected to the pleasure of being with children. Beach et al. (1998) also found that early childhood educators felt a relational commitment to the children and the profession.

The caregivers with whom I spoke enjoyed both the children and the relationships they developed. Reading some of the comments of the caregivers, Emma, a colleague and no longer working directly with children, agreed with their comments and said, "what I miss most about caregiving—the relationships."

Paying Attention to Emotions

Being a "special person" to a baby or a family is rewarding, and also involves being vulnerable to those particular people; when a caregiver is engaged so are her emotions. Saying good-bye to a young friend is sad; having a parent angry at you is frustrating; helping an emotionally distant parent acknowledge her child is overwhelming. Working in relationship means finding ways to connect despite anger, frustration, or overwhelming feelings. Saying good-bye fully, solving angry situations, naming over-whelming emotions can be unexpected satisfactions.

Too often, caregivers are given the message that there are "correct" emotions to feel; emotions must be controlled or regulated. Language such as "over-attached," "cares too much," "don't get too involved" all suggest that there is a correct amount of emotion. Once we care for someone and care about them, our heart is involved. We cannot measure the caring or the concern.

When we hold a baby close, smell the baby, feel that baby, we increasingly care about that baby. As shown in Hopkins's (1990) study of nursery nurses, when the nurses began to pay attention to the babies in their care and engaged with them, not only did the children acquire more language, but the nurses experienced more pleasure in their work with the children as well as more anxiety about the children. To have a relationship-based practice that is beneficial for children without having the emotions of being deeply committed to those children is not possible. Being in rela-tionship our emotions are engaged and need to be attended to.

Emotions can be signals; they can inform. Understanding the presence of an emotion, why it might be there and what it has to teach us, deepens our relationships and our practice. Feeling joy or anxiety, each can have a reason or meaning in a particular rela-tionship and in our lives. Relationships can unlock difficult, even devastating emotions. When caring for and about someone, their intereactions or their situations can affect us deeply. Understand-ing how we have been affected by a baby or a family and exploring that understanding does not stop the emotions but provides a path to working with them. Jade realizes that "emotions are all part of it. And I allow it. The clutter would be if I tried to block it."

When there is little or no support for the emotional work of caring for babies, caregivers may choose to not engage in relation-ships with children or families. Aware that the anticipated grief of saying good-bye or that the anger directed at a neglectful parent may be too much to bear, caregivers may choose not to invest themselves in authentic relationships. Yet the caregivers I interviewed had learned to deal with their emotions, with the support of co-workers and supervisors helping, as well as their own willingness to look inside themselves. Staying in touch with one's emotions can provide direction and guidance for solutions; when they are aware of their feelings, caregivers can then take responsibility for them. Working within the relationship, caregivers can understand what is possible for this child and family.

Process versus Product

If the practice of caring for infants and toddlers is relational, policy and guidelines cannot be prescriptive. Relationship cannot be mandated. Caregivers will connect with families and children in a manner unique to particular individuals and contexts. Relationships can be supported, emotions understood, situations reflected upon in an ongoing process.

Articulating the difference between valuing the work as relationship and valuing the work as product may help to focus the discussion about good practice. While reasonable ratios and group size are important as elements that may influence how relationships are fostered, they cannot in themselves indicate the quality of the relationship. Focusing on such measures can divert attention from developing and supporting the relationships in the practice. The rules and regulations of licensing or funding often create a template that does not fit each circumstance, resulting in care being seen as a product that is regulated rather than a process that changes with children, families, and caregivers. By focusing on the relationship, the process aspect of the work is highlighted and appreciated.

In this caring and relationship-centered process there is no certainty, and caregivers in this study spoke of living in ambiguity at times, wondering how to soothe an unhappy baby, soothe a parent's ruffled feathers, or help a frustrated toddler. Teaching students who have little experience in ECEC, I am aware of how intensely some look for the "correct method" to control a group of rowdy children or to catch the interest of the wandering child. Finding the best words or stance takes time and practice, and one is never completely sure that the "right" answer was found.

The words *attend* and *tension* have a common root, *tendere*, "to stretch" (Fowler and Fowler, 1964). When attentive, one is aware of tensions while stretching to be aware of the nuances in a person or situation. There are invariably challenging tensions within relationships as caregivers try to understand, respond, and balance the different bids for their attention, all making for a dynamic process. Caregivers in this study maintained relationships through an attentive presence, as through empathy and reflection they negotiated their connections to the children and families in their programs. They saw themselves as actively taking up the perspective and position of babies, parents, other staff members.

In British Columbia the structure of licensing does encourage centers to maintain some of the factors that could allow them to build positive connections. As we have seen, the institution-based program worked within the guidelines of licensing and followed the ratios and group sizes recommended by research to provide quality care, yet at this center there was a focus on caregiving as a product. The children were routines to be managed rather than individuals to be cared for and appreciated. In this center, Lynn struggled with the differences between what she had learned and the way care was managed. She acknowledged that having the infant-toddler training enabled her "to look at things in a different way." Within the culture of her center though, it was difficult to feel she was in a relationship with the families and children.

Government licensing sets the minimum standard below which centers cannot fall, yet care for infants and toddlers is expensive and centers need enough money to pay good staff and to hire enough staff. There should be enough resources for the supervisor to have adequate time to provide her staff with the neccessary guidance and support. The other programs in this study were well within the guidelines of licensing and yet went beyond the guidelines to institute practices that supported the process of developing relationships. These programs had even lower adult-child ratios, hired staff members with under three certificates, set time aside for meetings, and made qualified relief staff available. The value caregivers placed on the process of relating with babies, families, and co-workers was shared and supported by the workplace. Relationship-centered practice was supported by the programs with administrators who themselves had caring and thoughtful relationships with their staff.

Developmentally Appropriate Practice

The field of Early Childhood Education and Care has a long history. It is not the purpose of this book to go into the history of ECEC philosophy and ideas, but the research reported here takes place within the context of that history as it has developed over the last three hundred years (Mayfield, 2001; Williams and Fromberg, 1992).

Developmental psychology is a cornerstone of the last fifty years of ECEC (Lubeck, 1996). In British Columbia, for example, every ECEC program includes a course in child growth and development, while textbooks for the required course in the foundations of ECEC include a discussion of *developmentally appropriate practice* (DAP) (Gordon and Browne, 2000; Mayfield, 2001). Hunter and Gage (1998, p. 8), in *The Self-Assessment Workbook*, write, "knowledge of child growth and development is at the heart of the best practice in child care." According to Bredekamp and Copple (1997, p. 8), DAP programs are "based on what is known about how children develop and learn; such programs promote the development and enhance the learning of each individual child served."

Child development theory describes children in terms of their physical, cognitive, emotional, linguistic, and social growth. Growth is described in terms of the changes in these dimensions as seen at different ages. One expects a young infant (birth to nine months) to "delight in hearing language," to "learn through movement," and to "use their senses and emerging physical skills to learn about the people and objects around them" (Bredekamp and Copple, 1997, pp. 57–58). Each area of development has a set of skills associated with it at each age. As each age is characterized by a particular set of skills, a program can be generally geared to that age while paying attention to the unique interests of each child. Bredekamp (1987) developed guidelines for practice based on developmentally appropriate practice, and this concept has been taken up enthusiastically by the field. [*Zero to Three*, the National

Center for Infants, Toddlers and Families followed with their guidelines document, *Caring for Infants in Groups: Developmentally Appropriate Practice* (Lally et al., 1995)].

At present within the field, some of these ideas are under scrutiny and criticism because of their predominantly Eurocentric point of view (Cannella, 1997, 1998; Dahlberg, Moss, and Pence, 1999). There are several concerns. Traditionally, child development theory assumes a "universal child" (Lubeck, 1996) who will unfold in a fairly predictable manner given the correct circumstances. To a large degree, child development theories have been based on observations of middle-class white children (Katz, 1996), which Cannella (1997, p. 3) suggests has led to the silencing of "the actual children with whom we work as they live their real lives in settings that we have not comprehended, and as they display strengths and understandings that we have not dreamed of." Developmental guidelines also assume a progression toward a more preferred state, a more mature endpoint, for as Lubeck (1996, p. 157) suggests, child development theory is hierarchical, "moving from a less to a more adequate way of thinking." While assuming a universal child, the theory focuses on the progression of the individual child while paying little attention to the context of the child's social relations and material environment. Rogoff (1990), for example, draws our attention to the variety of ways infants begin to make meaning of the world. How an infant is held and talked to gives that infant a message about the world. Babies who are held facing the mother most of the time see the world differently than babies who are held to look out at the world. There are many paths to take in order to become an adult.

The discussion around child development theories is vibrant and lively. In 1996, the discussion was taken up by the journal *Early Childhood Research Quarterly* (Bowman and Stott, 1996; Katz, 1996; Lubeck, 1996). As Katz (1996, p. 136) says, she has been led to wonder if "mastery of child development knowledge and principles can contribute significantly and positively to competence in teaching and curriculum planning for young children." Lubeck (1996) feels that postmodernism has posed serious challenges to the assumptions of child development. She sees child development as a cultural construction, asking, "what are the effects, intended and unintended, of reducing a child to the one characteristic perceived by others to be a deficit, inadequacy or fault?" (p. 153). Bowman and Stott (1996, p. 196) suggest that child development is a "slippery base for practice." They encourage us to examine the developmental timetable and question its value for practice.

Tensions exist within the field since child development theory is questioned and critiqued, but not yet replaced, especially since much practical work has been built on these theories. Cannella (1998) draws our attention to the social construction of childhood and the child, the "construction of education for 'the child' resulting in the creation of the field of Early Childhood Education" (p. 158), and the creation of a profession that develops policy and practice regarding young children. New (1994, p. 69) is critical of the lack of representation in the child development research literature "of studies on culturally diverse populations." The studies that have been done, she goes on to say, present challenges to our "current beliefs regarding normative child development processes as well as optimal child development settings" (p. 69). She stresses that teachers and parents are also in a process of developing, and the ongoing development of adults is intertwined with the development of children.

This debate opens up possibilities for new strands of thinking, and as New (1994) says, we "can avoid the institutionalization of knowledge about childhood as we discover multiple possibilities for responding appropriately to young children's diverse competencies, needs, and potentials" (p. 79).

The concepts embedded in and elucidated by DAP were welcomed in the field as a clear statement of the principles of ECEC, yet later were to come under attack for being culturally bound and representative of the dominant discourse. For example, our society values independence and the individual, and we encourage our children to be independent individuals. "When asked who they are, they are expected to respond with individual identification (name and age) rather than with relational information (name and parents' names) as do the Mayan children with whom I worked," writes Rogoff (1990, p. 209).

Developmentally appropriate practice acknowledges the importance of responsive caregiving and supports the idea of one consistent, warm caregiver as being important for a child's early development. If the caregiving relationship between infant and caregiver is to be responsive, then it is crucial to uncover what *responsive* implies, especially as different cultures may have different understandings of what it means to respond to an infant.

While focusing on their relationship, the caregivers can use that relationship to try to understand the meaning of *responsive* for each family with whom they work. Developing an awareness of their own cultural roots will enable caregivers to stay cognizant of other approaches and values. The interviews in this study illustrated that to care for a baby warmly and thoughtfully, the caregiver must be woven into a web of relationships that engage her on many levels. With her own values, beliefs, and personal history, she enters into a unique relationship with each baby and family. She is influenced and affected, as is the baby, by their relationship with one another. Shifting the focus from the developmental appropriateness of responsive caregiving to the relationship with the baby and the other supporting relationships may make sense.

Jade acknowledged that she has moved beyond what she once deemed was "professional." She said, "if I have an emotional reaction, I allow it, even expressing anger, whereas before I would have held back and said 'no, that is not professional.' Now I don't always block that." Jade's expertise comes in knowing her emotions and deciding if it is possible and appropriate to express them. Expressing anger could be an unwise choice as it could leave a caregiver vulnerable to rejection, hostility, or anger. Yet it could also open doors to a deeper, new intimacy. Undertaking to make this choice with full understanding takes expertise and discernment.

The discussion of good practice must go beyond principles and practices based solely on theories of child development. Each child and each family presents its own special problem, and successful engagement demands the balancing of diverse needs, perspectives, and values. These need to be considered in the ongoing discussions as we prepare students for this work and support caregivers in their roles. We need an ongoing, evolving discourse. Katz (1996) reminds us, "the art of practice is not merely a means to an end or a search for solutions; rather it weaves means and ends, and the goal is to transform through understanding" (p. 146). We can learn from each other, and as Susan Bernheimer (2003) says, "The greatest challenge of our time is developing the skill to live with purpose in the face of upheaval and uncertainty. Inherent in this skill is an ability to fully embrace our lives with all their complexity and contradictions. It necessitates finding ways of expanding beyond the safety of our old beliefs and building our capacity to empathize with others" (p. 54).

The Role of the ECEC Educator

The education and training of students in an infant-toddler ECEC program happens within a relationship. Teacher and student each affect and are affected by their relationships with one another. Perhaps it is within these relationships that we, as teachers, can have the most impact. Several years ago, while working at a community college, I struggled with course outlines. The mandate was to convey the precise nature of the goals of the course and to convey what observable behaviors by the students would result in a specific course grade. I felt this would be appropriate for a math course or physics course, but I was teaching Art for Preschoolers. How would I evaluate students' experience with the materials and ideas? While some students moved with confidence in this area, others lived with the memory of a kindergarten teacher who had quashed their enthusiasm. I believed that enjoyment of the materials and the process itself were key to students' learning how to engage in creative work with the children. Some students had longer learning journeys than others; grading focused on their performance as product rather than as process.

I was concerned about the students' relationship to art materials and about their own memories of participating in art. I felt I had to model my own joy in the process and to encourage each student to explore her own relationship to art as I felt that encouraging their genuine involvement with the materials would lead them into a more dynamic process with the children when exploring art materials. Yonemura (1994) said of teaching new teachers, "All children need teachers who reject sentimentality and attend to their emotions, young children especially because they are particularly vulnerable during these early years when they must cope with a complex world at a time of great dependency in their development. Teachers need support in recognizing and coping with their own feelings if they are to accomplish such demanding work. I believe that I must attend to my students' feelings if I am to be effective at my work" (p. 170).

Just as ECEC students should look at each young child as unique and full of possibilities, so too we must connect with each student to help him or her realize his or her capacity. Ayers (1993) says, "The dizzying diversity of human experience and capacity alone demands that teachers look deeply at our students, that we see them as creatures like ourselves, and yet unique in important ways. This is a central challenge of teaching, and it is essentially a moral challenge; it cannot be resolved by referring to fact or to empirical data alone. There is no single, provable answer" (p. 21).

It is not always possible to know the journey a student is on any more than we can know what is in store for a baby or toddler, but we can connect with each student and honor the possibilities. We can model in our relationship with them the qualities we hope they will take to their connections with children and families: respect, responsiveness, and caring.

I have learned to pay attention to the process and the participants from my discussions with the caregivers, and found my own teaching affected. I have tried to remain responsive to the moment. A few months after I finished my interviews, I recorded this encounter with a new group of ECEC students:

> "Those theorists," says one of the Early Childhood Education students I am teaching, "seems to me what they're saying is just common sense."
>
> I have been trying to start a discussion about the theories and ideas on which Early Childhood Education is built. No one is very interested.
>
> Instead, the conversation switches to a question in the coursework: What would different theorists advise parents to do whose child would not sleep through the night in her own crib?
>
> "I just couldn't get my head around this question at all, says another student. My son sleeps with me and my sister's son sleeps with her. I asked my mother and my auntie and they didn't know."
>
> Other students in this small class of eight chimed in.

We have moved from the tenuous ground of the theorists to the knowledge of known people, people one has a relationship with and who have authority in these women's lives. Stories begin to be told about what happens in each family. There is an unspoken consensus that they would advise taking the baby to the parents' bed. They are uncertain about what advice they would give for sleeping in the crib.

In an attempt to return the conversation to the theorists I try to explain the work of theorists. "Those fellows have made up stories to explain what they have seen or experienced in their lives." That seemed to make them seem more approachable, and we moved back to Piaget, Vygotsky, and Erikson and left the question of the crib.

These women trusted the people they had relationships with for answers about child care. The theorists seemed distant to them. Relationship is a powerful force. Like the caregivers, I like the relationships that are part of teaching. Teaching is filled with a web of connections—theory, practice, students, children, babies, practicum supervisors.

My teaching is about relationship, connection to students, connection to material, connection to children, connection to ideas. Entering into relationship with students, I feel I am on a journey that forges its own course and demands its own time. Opportunities to understand a student's reality and perceptions allow me to respond in a congruent manner: congruent to the material, and congruent, I hope, with a student's perspective. This journey always includes dead ends, false starts, unexpected surprises, uphill climbs, and breathtaking views.

The journey does take time: I must wait for the right moment and must match my pace to the student's pace. Within a safe relationship built over time, children and adults will take risks in thought and action—and so will teachers. The research relationship meant honoring the connections my participants had with their practice, my own connections with the practice, and my connections with each of these women. Through careful attention our relationships emerged and grew in unexpected ways and directions. Thinking of ourselves as in relationship encourages us to be careful and caring. Mary Catherine Bateson (2000) says, "the gift of personhood is potentially present in every human interaction, every time we touch or speak or call one another by name, yet denial can be very subtle too, inflicted in the failure to listen, to empathize, to attend" (p. 62).

Conclusion

All the caregivers took a thoughtful and respectful approach to the infants in their care. They used mindfulness, empathy, and relationships with others to inform their practice. Although they had in common an ECEC course focused on infants and toddlers, these caregivers took their experiences and distilled them through their own belief systems and personal histories before evolving a personal style that was reflected in their relationships with the babies and parents.

Although they participate in a society that often thinks of caregivers' work as babysitting, and caregivers' work is characterized by low wages and status, the women in this study still believe in the importance of what they do. As of 2005, Jade, Rachel, Sheryl, and Lynn continue to work with babies. Dawn and Mary have taken time away from work to look after their own children. Mel is finishing a nursing degree and has adopted a child.

All of these caregivers offered their narratives generously. While each caregiver is in the midst of her own history of connection and community, a baby is at the beginning of her or his own story of connection within community. How caregivers of infants and toddlers handle their connections with young children and their families has an impact. Bateson (1994) says, "personhood arises from a long process of welcoming closeness and continues to grow and require nourishment over a lifetime of participation" (p. 62).

I have been hesitant to offer strong recommendations, not because I do not feel strongly, but because I would prefer to offer these stories and voices for discussion and for thought. This has been a process of uncovering the thoughts of the caregivers, as well as my own. The value is found within the process and I urge others to embark upon it.

Notes

Chapter 1. Relationship with Baby

1. Hrdy (1999) defines this term as "all care takers other than the mother who help care for or provision the young."

2. Most infant-toddler caregivers in Canada are female; the pronoun *she* will be used here.

3. All names used in this study, including those of children, are pseudonyms. Each participant has her own pseudonym.

Chapter 4. The Public Story of Caregiving

1. According to archaeologists, the name of the Egyptian princess who rescued Moses was Thermutis, daughter of Queen Alfat'anit. But this name is never mentioned in the Hebrew Bible.

Chapter 6. Responsive Caregiving

1. The British Columbia child care regulations mandate a 4:1 ratio, and this center was in compliance with this ratio. The other centers had decided to have a lower ratio of 3:1, which is suggested by the British Columbia regulations.

Works Cited

Abram, David. 1996. *The spell of the sensuous: Perception and language in a more-than-human world*. New York: Pantheon Books.

Ainsworth, Mary D. 1962. *Infancy in Uganda: Infant care and the growth of love*. Baltimore: Johns Hopkins University Press.

———. 1964. Patterns of attachment behavior shown by the infant in interaction with his mother. *Merrill-Palmer Quarterly* 10 (1):51–58.

Ainsworth, Mary D., and Silva M. Bell. 1977. Infant crying and maternal responsiveness: A rejoinder to Gewirtz and Boyd. *Child Development* 48:1208–1216.

Ainsworth, Mary D., and Silvia M. Bell. 1970. Attachment, exploration, and separation: Illustrated by the behavior of one-year-olds in a strange situation. *Child Development* 41A (1):49–67.

Ainsworth, Mary D., Silvia M. Bell, and Donelda J. Stayton. 1972. Individual differences in the development of some attachment behaviors. *Merrill-Palmer Quarterly* 18:123–143.

Ainsworth, Mary D., M. C. Blehar, E. Waters, and S. Wall. 1978. *Patterns of attachment: A psychological study of the strange situation*. Hillside, NJ: Lawrence Erlbaum Associates.

Ames, Eleanor. 1997. The development of Romanian orphanage children adopted in Canada. Burnaby, BC: Simon Fraser University.

Attridge, C. and M. Callahan, 1987. Women in Women's Work: Nurses' perspective of quality work environments. Research Report #1. Victoria, B.C.: University of Victoria.

Ayers, William. 1991. Teaching and being: Connecting teachers' accounts of their lives with classroom practice. In *Critical perspec-

tives on early childhood education, edited by L. Weis, P. G. Altbach, G. P. Kelly, and H. G. Petrie. Albany, NY: State University of New York Press.

———. 1993. *To teach: The journey of a teacher.* New York: Teachers College Press.

Barone, Tom E. 1990. Using the narrative text as an occasion for conspiracy. In *Qualitative inquiry in education: The continuing debate*, edited by E. W. Eisner and A. Peshkin. New York: Teachers College Press.

———. 2001. Science, art, and the predispositions of educational researchers. *Educational Researcher* 30 (7):24–28.

Bateson, Mary Catherine. 1984. *With a daughter's eye: A memoir of Margaret Mead and Gregory Bateson.* New York: Washington Square Press.

———. 1994. *Peripheral visions: Learning along the way.* New York: Harper Collins.

———. 2000. *Full circles, overlapping lives: Culture and generation in transition.* New York: Ballantine Books.

Beach, Jane, Jane Bertrand, and Gordon Cleveland. 1998. *Our child care workforce: From recognition to remuneration, more than a labour of love.* Ottawa: Human Resource Development Canada.

Beach, Jane, Bosica Costigliola, Jane Bertrand, Barry Forer, Donna Michal, and Jocelyne Tougas. 2004. *Working for change: Canada's child care workforce.* Ottawa: Child Care Human Resources Sector Council.

Behar, Ruth. 1996. *The vulnerable observer: Anthropology that breaks your heart.* Boston: Beacon Press.

Belenky, Mary Field, Lynne A. Bond, and Jacqueline S. Weinstock. 1997. *A tradition that has no name: Nurturing the development of people, families, and communities.* New York: Basic Books.

Belenky, Mary Field, B. M. Clinchy, N. R. Goldberger, and J. M. Tarule. 1986. *Women's ways of knowing: The development of self, voice, and mind.* New York: Basic Books.

Belsky, Jay, and Michael J. Rovine. 1988. Nonmaternal care in the first year of life and the security of infant-parent attachment. *Child Development* 59:157–167.

Benner, Alison. 1999. Quality child care and community development: What is the connection? In *Research connections Canada: Supporting children and families*, edited by S. Sullivan, K. Bose, and L. Levesque. Ottawa: Canadian Child Care Federation.

Benner, P., and S. Gordon. 1996. Caring practice. In *Caregiving, readings in knowledge, practice, ethics and politics*, edited by P. Benner and N. Noddings. Philadelphia: University of Pennsylvania Press.

Benner, P., and J. Wrubel. 1989. *The primacy of caring, stress and coping in health and illness*. San Francisco: Addison-Wesley.

Bernhardt, J. L. 2000. A primary caregiving system for infants and toddlers: Best for everyone involved. *Young Children* 55 (2):74–80.

Bernheimer, Susan. 2003. *New possibilities for Early Childhood Education: Stories from our nontraditional students*. Los Angeles: Peter Lang.

Bowden, Peta. 1997. *Caring: Gender-sensitive ethics*. London: Routledge.

Bowlby, John. 1951. *Maternal care and mental health*. Vol. 2, *World Health Organization Monograph Series*. Geneva: World Health Organization.

———. 1973. *Separation: Anxiety and anger*. Vol. 2, *Attachment and loss*. Harmondsworth, England: Penguin Books.

———. 1978. *Attachment*. 2nd ed. Vol. 1, *Attachment and loss*. London: Penguin Books.

———. 1991. *The making and breaking of affectional bonds*. New York: Routledge.

Bowman, Barbara, and Frances Stott. 1996. Child development knowledge: A slippery base for practice. *Early Childhood Research Quarterly* 11:169–183.

Brazelton, T. Berry. 1983. *Infants and mothers*. 2nd ed. New York: Dell Publishing.

Brazelton, T. Berry, and Bertrand Cramer. 1990. *The earliest relationship: Parents, infants, and the drama of early attachment*. Reading, MA: Addison-Wesley.

Brazelton, T. Berry, Barbara Koslowski, and Mary Main. 1974. The origin of reciprocity: The early mother-infant interaction. In *The effect of the infant on its caregiver*, edited by M. Lewis and L. A. Rosenblum. New York: John Wiley & Sons.

Bredekamp, Sue, ed. 1987. *Developmentally appropriate practice in early childhood programs serving children from birth through age eight.* Washington, DC: National Association for the Education of Young Children.

Bredekamp, Sue, and Carol Copple, eds. 1997. *Developmentally appropriate practice in early childhood programs.* Revised edition. Washington, DC: National Association for the Education of Young Children.

Bruer, J. T. 1999. *The myth of the first three years.* New York: Free Press.

Calhoun, Cheshire. 1992. Emotional work. In *Explorations in feminist ethics*, edited by E. B. Cole and S. Coultrap-McQuin. Bloomington, IN: Indiana University Press.

Canadian Child Care Federation. 1992. *Caring for a living.* Ottawa: Canadian Child Care Federation/Canadian Child Care Advocacy Association.

Cannella, Gaile S. 1997. *Deconstructing early childhood education: Social justice and revolution.* Edited by J. L. Kincheloe and J. Jipson. Vol. 2, *Rethinking Childhood.* New York: Peter Lang.

———. 1998. Early childhood education: A call for the construction of revolutionary images. In *Curriculum toward new identities*, edited by W. Pinar. New York: Garland.

Cannella, Gaile S., and Joe L. Kincheloe, eds. 2002. *Kidworld: Childhood studies, gobal perspectives, and education.* New York: Peter Lang.

Carlson, Frances M. 2005. Significance of touch in young children's lives. *Young Children* 60 (4):79–85.

Casper, V. 1996. Making familiar unfamiliar and unfamiliar familiar. *Zero to Three* 16 (3):14–20.

Chess, S., A. Thomas, and H. G. Birch. 1965. *Your child is a person: A psychological approach to parenthood without guilt.* New York: Viking Press.

Childcare Resource and Research Unit. 2000. *Early childhood education and care in Canada: Provinces and territories: 1998.* Toronto: Childcare Resource and Research Unit, University of Toronto.

Chisholm, Kim, Margaret C. Carter, Elinor W. Ames, and Sara J. Morrison. 1995. Attachment security and indiscriminately friendly behavior in children adopted from Romanian orphanages. *Development and Psychopathology* 7:283–294.

Chisholm, Kim. 1995. Orientation talk to prospective parents of international adoptees. Paper read at Attachment: Implications for infant-toddler caregivers, at Victoria, BC.

Clarke-Stewart, Alison. 1992. Consequences of child care for children's development. In *Child care in the 1990s: Trends and consequences*, edited by A. Booth. Hillsdale, NJ: Lawrence Erlbaum Associates.

Cleveland, G., and M. Krashinsky. 1998. *The benefits and costs of good child care: The economic rationale for public investment in young children*. Toronto: Childcare Resource and Research Unit, Centre for Urban & Community Studies, University of Toronto.

Clifford, James. 1986. Introduction: Partial truths. In *Writing culture: The poetics and politics of ethnography*, edited by J. Clifford and G. Marcus. Berkeley, CA: University of California Press.

Clinchy, B. M. 1996. Connected and separate knowing: Toward a marriage of two minds. In *Knowledge, difference, and power: Essays inspired by Women's Ways of Knowing*, edited by N. Goldberger, J. Tarule, B. M. Clinchy, and M. Belenky. New York: Basic Books.

Cole, Eve Browning, and Susan Coultrap-McQuin, eds. 1992. *Explorations in feminist ethics: Theory and practice*. Bloomington, IN: Indiana University Press.

Connelly, F. Michael, and D. Jean Clandinin. 1990. Stories of experience and narrative inquiry. *Educational Researcher* 19 (5):2–14.

Corso, R. 2003. The center on the social and emotional foundations for early learning. *Young Children* 58 (4):46–47.

Cuffaro, Harriet K. 1995. *Experimenting with the world: John Dewey and the early childhood classroom*. New York: Teachers College Press.

Culkin, Mary L., ed. 2000. *Managing quality in young children's programs: The leader's role*. New York: Teachers College Press.

Dahlberg, Gunilla, Peter Moss, and Alan Pence. 1999. *Beyond quality in early childhood education and care*. London: Falmer Press.

Damasio, Antonio. 1999. *The feeling of what happens: Body and emotion in the making of consciousness*. New York: Harcourt.

Delpit, Lisa. 1995. *Other people's children: Cultural conflict in the classroom*. New York: The New Press.

Doherty, Gillian. 1999a. Elements of quality. In *Research connections Canada: Supporting children and families*, edited by S. Sullivan, K. Bose, and L. Levesque. Ottawa: Canadian Child Care Federation.

———. 1999b. Multiple stakeholders: multiple perspectives. In *Research connections Canada: Supporting children and families*, edited by S. Sullivan, K. Bose, and L. Levesque. Ottawa: Canadian Child Care Federation.

———. 2001. *Targeting early childhood care and education: Myths and realities.* Toronto: Childcare Resource and Research Unit, Centre for Urban and Community Studies, University of Toronto.

Doherty, Gillian, and Barry Forer. 2005. *Shedding new light on staff recruitment and retention: Challenges in child care.* Ottawa, Ontario: Child Care Human Resources Sector Council.

Doherty, Gillian, Donna S. Lero, Hillel Goelman, Annette LaGrange, and Jocelyne Tougas. 2000. *You bet I care! A Canada-wide study on wages, working conditions, and practices in child care centres.* Guelph: Centre for Families, Work, and Well-Being.

Donawa, M. W. 1999. *A rebel band of friends: Understanding through women's narratives of friendship, identity, and moral agency.* Interdisciplinary, Ph.D dissertation, University of Victoria, Victoria, BC.

Dreyfus, H., and S. Dreyfus. 1985. *Mind over machine: The power of human intuition and expertise in the era of the computer.* New York: Free Press.

Elliot, Enid, ed. 1995. *An introduction to attachment theory.* Victoria, BC: Girls' Alternative Program.

Erikson, Erik H. 1950. Growth and crises of the healthy personality. In *Symposium on the healthy personality*, edited by M.J.E. Senn. New York: Josiah Macey Jr. Foundation.

Eyer, Diane. 1992. *Mother-infant bonding: A scientific fiction.* New Haven: Yale University Press.

———. 1996. *Motherguilt: How our culture blames mothers for what's wrong.* New York: Times Books.

Fancourt, R. 2000. Brain development and learning. *The First Years: New Zealand Journal of Infant and Toddler Education* 2 (2):22–26.

Farquhar, Sarah-Eve. 2000. Re-valuing physical contact with young children. *The First Years: New Zealand Journal of Infant and Toddler Education* 2 (2):5–9.

Fein, Gret G., Antonio Garibaldi, and Raffaella Boni. 1993. The adjustment of infants and toddlers to group care: The first 6 months. *Early Childhood Research Quarterly* 8:1–14.

Fitzgerald, F. Scott. 1963. The crack-up. In *The Fitzgerald Reader*, edited by A. Mizener. New York: Charles Scribner's Sons.

Fleming, Alison, Carl Carter, Joy Stallings, and Meir Steiner. 2002. Testoserone and prolactin are associated with emotional responses to infant cries in new fathers. *Hormones and Behavior* 42 (4):399–413.

Fowler, H. W., and F. G. Fowler, eds. 1964. *The concise Oxford dictionary*. 5th ed. Oxford: Clarendon Press.

Gerber, Magda, ed. 1979. *Manual for parents and professionals*. Los Angeles: Resources for Infant Educarers.

Gerber, Magda, and Allison Johnson. 1998. *Your self-confident baby: How to encourage your child's natural abilities—from the very start*. New York: John Wiley & Sons.

Gerstenzang, Sarah. 2005. Attachment: Meeting the eyes of love. *Zero to Three* 25 (5):54–57.

Gilligan, Carol. 1982. *In a different voice: Psychological theory and women's development*. Cambridge, MA: Harvard University Press.

Gilligan, Carol, and Grant Wiggins. 1988. The origins of morality in early childhood relationships. In *Mapping the moral domain: A contribution of women's thinking to psychological theory and education*, edited by C. Gilligan, J. V. Ward and J. M. Taylor. Cambridge, MA: Harvard University Press.

Gladwell, Malcolm. 1997. Damaged. *The New Yorker*, Feb. 24, 132–147.

Goelman, Hillel, and Alan Pence. 1987. Effects of child care, family, and individual characteristics on children's language development: The Victoria day care research project. In *Quality in child care: What does research tell us?* edited by D. Philips. Washington, DC: National Association of Young Children.

Goffin, Stacie G., and David E. Day, eds. 1994. *New perspectives in early childhood teacher education: Bringing practitioners into the debate*. New York: Teachers College Press.

Goldstein, Lisa. 1997. *Teaching with love: A feminist approach to early childhood education*. Edited by J. L. Kincheloe and J. Jipson. Vol. 1, *Rethinking childhood*. New York: Peter Lang.

Goleman, Daniel. 1998. *Working with emotional intelligence*. New York: Bantam.

Gonzalez-Mena, Janet, and Dianne Widmeyer Eyer. 1989. *Infants, toddlers, and caregivers*. Mountain View, CA: Mayfield Publishing.

———. 2001. *Infants, toddlers, and caregivers*. 5th ed. Mountain View, CA: Mayfield Publishing.

Gordon, A. M., and K. W. Browne. 2000. *Beginnings and beyond*. 5th ed. Albany, NY: Delmar.

Gordon, Suzanne. 1996. Feminism and caring. In *Caregiving: Readings in practice, ethics, and politics*, edited by S. Gordon, P. Benner, and N. Noddings. Philadelphia: University of Pennsylvania Press.

Gottlieb, Alma. 2004. *The afterlife is where we come from: The culture of infancy in West Africa*. 1st ed. Chicago and London: University of Chicago.

Greene, Maxine. 1990. The tensions and passions of caring. In *The caring imperative in education*, edited by M. M. Leininger and J. Watson. New York: NLN.

Greenough, W. T. 1990. Brain Storage of information from cutaneous and other modalites. In *Touch: The foundation of experience,* edited by K. E. Barnard and T. B. Brazelton. Madison, WI: International Universities Press, Inc.

Grumet, Madeleine. 1988. *Bitter milk: Women and teaching*. Amherst: University of Massachusetts Press.

Gunnar, M. R., L. Brodersen, K. Krueger, and R. Rigatuso. 1996. Dampening of behavioral and adrenocortical reactivity during early infancy: Normative changes and individual differences. *Child Development* 67 (3):877–89.

Hallie, Philip. 1979. *Lest innocent blood be shed*. London: Michael Joseph.

———. 1997. *Tales of good and evil, help and harm*. New York: Harper Collins Publishers.

Hamilton, Claire. 1994. Moving beyond an initial level of competence as an infant teacher. In *New perspectives in early childhood teacher education: Bringing practitioners into the debate*, edited by S. Goffin and D. Day. New York: Teachers College Press.

Hatch, J. A. 1995. Studying childhood as a cultural invention: A rationale and framework. In *Qualitative research in early childhood settings*, edited by J. A. Hatch. Westport, CT: Praeger.

Hauser, M., and J. A. Jipson, eds. 1998. *Intersections: Feminisims and early childhoods.* Vol. 3. New York: Peter Lang.

Hochschild, A. 1983. *The managed heart: Commercialization of human feeling.* Berkeley: University of California Press.

Hofferth, S. L. 1992. Demand for and supply of child care in the 1990s. In *Child care in the 1990s: Trends and consequences,* edited by A. Booth. Hillsdale, NJ: Lawrence Erlbaum Associates.

Hopkins, Juliet. 1990. Facilitating the development of intimacy between nurses and infants in day nurseries. In *Optimizing early child care and education,* edited by A. S. Honig. New York: Gordon and Breach Science Publishers.

Howe, Nina, and Ellen Jacobs. 1995. Child care research: A case for Canadian national standards. *Canadian Psychology* 36 (2):131–148.

Howes, Carollee, and Claire E. Hamilton. 1993. Child care for young children. In *Handbook of research on the education of young children,* edited by B. Spodek. New York: Macmillan.

———. 1993. The changing experience of child care: Changes in teachers and in teacher-child relationships and children's social competence with peers. *Early Childhood Research Quarterly* 8:15–32.

Howes, Carollee, Deborah A. Phillips, and Marcy Whitebrook. 1992. Thresholds of quality: Implications for the social development of children in center-based child care. *Child Development* 63:449-460.

Howes, Carollee, and Ellen W. Smith. 1995. Relations among child care quality, teacher behavior, children's play activities, emotional security, and cognitive activity in child care. *Early Childhood Research Quarterly* 10 (3):381–404.

Hrdy, Sarah Blaffer. 1999. *Mother Nature: A history of mothers, infants and natural selection.* New York: Pantheon Books.

Huebner, Dwayne E. 1999. Spirituality and Knowing. In *The lure of the transcendent: Collected essays by Dwayne E. Huebner,* edited by V. Hillis. Mahwah, NJ: Lawrence Erlbaum Associates.

Hunter, Theresa, and Susan Gage. 1998. *The self-assessment workbook: An evaluation tool kit for child care providers.* Vancouver, BC: Early Childhood Educators of British Columbia.

Insel, Thomas R. 2000. Toward a neurobiology of attachment. *Review of General Psychology* 4 (2):176–185.

Jayapal, Pramila. 2000. *Pilgrimage: One woman's return to a changing India.* Seattle, WA: Seal Press.

Jones, E. and G. Reynolds, 1992. *The play's the thing: Teachers' roles in children's play.* New York: Teachers College Press.

Jordan, Judith, Alexandra G. Kaplan, Jean Baker Miller, Irene P. Stiver, and Janet L. Surrey. 1991. *Women's growth in connection: Writings from the stone center.* New York and London: Guilford Press.

Jorde-Bloom, P. 1988. *A great place to work: Improving conditions for staff in young children's programs.* Washington, DC: National Association for the Education of Young Children.

Josselson, Ruthellen. 1995. Imagining the real: Empathy, narrative and the dialogic self. In *Interpreting experience: The narrative study of lives,* edited by A. Lieblich. Thousand Oaks, CA: Sage Publications.

Kagan, Jerome. 1978. *Infancy: Its place in human development.* Cambridge, MA: Harvard University Press.

———. 1984. *The nature of the child.* New York: Basic Books.

Kaplan, Louise. 1995. *No voice is ever wholly lost.* New York: Simon and Schuster.

Karen, Robert. 1994. *Becoming attached.* New York: Warner Books.

Katz, Lilian G. 1996. Child development knowledge and teacher preparation: Confronting assumptions. *Early Childhood Research Quarterly* 11:135–146.

Kegan, Robert. 1982. *The evolving self: Problem and process in human development.* Cambridge, MA and London, England: Harvard University Press.

Kestenberg-Amighi, Janet. 2004. Contact and connection: A cross-cultural look at parenting styles in Bali and the United States. *Zero to Three* 24 (5):32–39.

Kohlberg, Lawrence. 1971. Stages of moral development as a basis for moral education. In *Moral education: Interdisciplinary approaches,* edited by C. Beck, B. S. Crittenden, and E. V. Sullivan. Toronto: University of Toronto Press.

———. 1981. *The philosophy of moral development.* San Francisco: Harper and Row.

Kottler, Jeffrey A. 1993. *On being a therapist.* San Francisco: Jossey-Bass.

Lagerway, Mary. 1998. *Reading Auschwitz*. Walnut Creek, CA: AltaMira Press.

Lally, J. Ronald. 1995. The impact of child care policies and practices on infant toddler identity formation. *Young Children* 51 (1):58–66.

Lally, J. Ronald, and S. Gilford. 1996. *Protective urges: Working with the feelings of parents and caregivers*. Sacramento, CA: [West Ed: The Program for Infant Toddler Caregivers.] Video.

Lally, J. Ronald, Abbey Griffin, Emily Fenichel, Marilyn Segal, Eleanor Szanton, and Bernice Weissbourd. 1995. *Caring for infants and toddlers in groups: Developmentally appropriate practice*. Washington, DC: Zero to Three.

Lally, J. Ronald, and Helen Keith. 1997. Early head start: The first two years. *Zero to Three* 18 (2):3–8.

Lama, His Holiness the Dalai, and Howard C. Cutler. 1998. *The art of happiness: A handbook for living*. New York: Riverhead Books.

Langer, Ellen. 1989. *Mindfulness*. Reading, MA: Addison-Wesley.

Leavitt, Robin Lynn. 1994. *Power and emotion in infant-toddler day care*. Albany, NY: State University of New York Press.

———. 1995. The emotional culture of infant-toddler day care. In *Qualitative research in early childhood settings*, edited by J. A. Hatch. Westport, CT: Praeger.

Lee, Debra. 2000. Myths or realities? Some thoughts about settling infants into early childhood centres. *The First Years: New Zealand Journal of Infant and Toddler Education* 2 (1):13–15.

Lero, D. S., A. R. Pence, M. Shields, L. M. Brockman, and H. Goelman. 1992. *Canadian national child care study: Introductory report*. Ottawa: Statistics Canada and Health and Welfare Canada.

Lieberman, Alicia F. 1993. *The emotional life of the toddler*. New York: The Free Press.

Light, K. C., Tara Smith, J. M. Johns, K. A. Brownley, and J. A. Hofheimer. 2000. Oxytocin responsivity in mothers of infants: A preliminary study of relationships with blood pressure during laboratory stress and normal ambulatory activity. *Health Psychology* 19 (6):560–567.

Lubeck, Sally. 1985. *Sandbox Society: Early education in black and white America*. London: The Falmer Press.

Lubeck, Sally. 1996. Deconstructing "child development knowledge" and "teacher preparation." *Early Childhood Research Quarterly* 11:147–167.

Mahoney, Michael. 1996. Connected knowing in constructive psychotherapy. In *Knowledge, difference, and power: Essays inspired by Women's Ways of Knowing*, edited by N. Goldberger, J. Tarule, B. Clinchy, and M. Belenky. New York: Basic Books.

Main, Mary, N. Kaplan, and J. Cassidy. 1985. Security in infancy, childhood and adulthood: A move to the level of representation. In *Growing points in attachment theory and research*, edited by I. Bretherton and E. Waters: Monographs of the Society for Research in Child Development. 50:66–104.

Main, Mary, and Donna R. Weston. 1981. The quality of the toddler's relationship to mother and father: Related to conflict behavior and the readiness to establish new relationship. *Child Development* 52:932–940.

Mann, Tammy. 1997. Promoting the mental health of infants and toddlers in early Head Start. *Zero to Three* 18 (2):37–40.

Manning, R. 1992. Just caring. In *Explorations in feminist ethics*, edited by E. B. Cole and S. Coultrap-McQuin. Indianapolis: Indiana University Press.

Marcus, G. F., S. Vijayan, S. Bandi Rao, and P. M. Vishton. 1999. Rule learning by seven-month-old infants. *Science* 283:77–80.

Marris, Peter. 1993. The social construction of uncertainty. In *Attachment across the life cycle*, edited by C. Parkes, J. Stevenson-Hinde, and P. Marris. London and New York: Routledge.

Mayfield, Margie I. 2001. *Early childhood education and care in Canada: Contexts, dimensions, and issues*. Toronto: Prentice Hall.

Meloy, Judith. 1994. *Writing the qualitative dissertation: Understanding by doing*. Hillsdale, NJ: Lawrence Erlbaum Associates.

Miller, J. B., and I. P. Stiver. 1997. *The healing connection: How women form relationships in therapy and life*. Boston: Beacon Press.

Moberg, Kerstin U. 2003. *The oxytocin factor: Tapping the hormone of calm, love, and healing*. Cambridge: Da Capo Press.

Montagu, A. 1971. *Touching: The human significance of the skin*. New York: Harper and Row.

Muir, Elisabeth E., and Eyglo Thorlaksdottir. 1992. Psychotherapeutic intervention with mothers and children in day care. *American Journal of Orthopsychiatry* 64 (1):60–67.

Munro, Petra. 1998. *Subject to fiction: Women teachers' life history narratives and the cultural politics of resistance*. Philadelphia: Open University Press.

Nelson, Margaret K. 1990. Mothering others' children: The experience of family day-care providers. *Sign: Journal of Women in Culture and Society* 15 (3): 586–605.

New, Rebecca S. 1994. Culture, child development, and developmentally appropriate practices: Teachers as collaborative researchers. In *Diversity and developmentally appropriate practices: Challenges for early childhood education*, edited by B. L. Mallory and R. S. New. New York: Teachers College Press.

Newberger, Julie J. 1997. New brain development research—a wonderful window of opportunity to build public support for early childhood education. *Young Children* 52 (4):4–9.

Noddings, Nel. 1984. *Caring: A feminine approach to ethics and moral education*. Berkeley: University of California Press.

———. 1996. The cared-for. In *Caregiving: Readings in knowledge, practice, ethics, and politics*, edited by S. Gordon, P. Benner, and N. Noddings. Philadelphia: University of Pennsylvania Press.

Nouwen, Henri J. M. 1975. *Reaching out: The three movements of the spiritual life*. New York: Doubleday.

Oxenhandler, Noelle. 2001. *The eros of parenthood: Explorations in light and dark*. New York: St. Martin's Press.

Palacio-Quintin, E. 2000. The impact of day care on child development. *Isuma* 1 (2):17–22.

Paley, Vivian Gussin. 1979. *White teacher*. Cambridge, MA: Harvard University Press.

———. 1986. *Boys and Girls: Superheroes in the doll corner*. Chicago: University of Chicago Press.

———. 1990. *The boy who would be a helicopter*. Cambridge, MA: Harvard University Press.

———. 1992. *You can't say you can't play*. Cambridge, MA: Harvard University Press.

———. 1995. *Kwanzaa and me: A teacher's story*. Cambridge, MA: Harvard University Press.

———. 1997. *The girl with the brown crayon*. Cambridge, MA: Harvard University Press.

Palmer, Parker. 1983. *To know as we are known: A spirituality of education*. San Francisco: Harper Collins.

———. 2000. *Let your life speak: Listening for the voice of vocation*. San Francisco: John Wiley and Sons.

Pawl, Jeree, and Maria St. John. 1998. *How you are is as important as what you do . . . in making a positive difference for infants, toddlers, and their families*. Washington, DC: Zero to Three.

Pence, Alan R., and Allison Benner. 2000. Child care research in Canada, 1965–99. In *Early childhood care and education in Canada*, edited by L. Prochner and N. Howe. Vancouver, BC: UBC Press.

Penn, Helen. 1999. *How should we care for babies and toddlers? An analysis of practice in out-of-home care for children under three*. Toronto: Childcare Resource and Research Unit, Centre for Urban & Community Studies, University of Toronto.

Perry, Bruce D. 1993. Neurodevelopment and the neurophysiology of trauma. *The APSAC Advisor* 6 (1 & 2).

———. 1999. Effects of traumatic events on children, an introduction. *Interdisciplinary Education Series Child Trauma Academy* 2 (3): pp. 12–20.

———. 2004. Maltreatment and Attachment: A Neurodevelopmental Perspective. Paper read at The Early Years, 2001. Vancouver, BC.

Phillips, Deborah A., ed. 1987. *Quality in child care: What does research tell us?* Vol. 1, *Research monographs of the National Association for the Education of Young Children*. Washington, DC: National Association for Young Children.

Pikler, Emmi. 1979. A quarter of a century of observing infants in a residential center. In *A manual for parents and professionals: Resources for infant educarers*, edited by M. Gerber. Los Angeles: Resources for Infant Educarers.

Polanyi, Michael. 1958. *Personal knowledge: Towards a post-critical philosophy*. Chicago: University of Chicago Press.

Polkinghorne, Donald E. 1988. *Narrative knowing and the human sciences*. New York: State University of New York Press.

Posada, German, Amanda Jacobs, Melissa Richmond, Olga Carbonell, Gloria Alzate, Maria Bustamante, and Julio Quiceno. 2002. Maternal caregiving and infant security in two cultures. *Developmental Psychology* 38 (1):67–78.

Prochner, Larry. 1996. Quality of care in historical perspective. *Early Childhood Research Quarterly* 11:5–17.

———. 2003. The American crèche: "Let's do what the French do, but do it our way." *Contemporary Issues in Early Childhood* 4 (3):267–285.

Provence, Sally. 1974. A program of group day care for young children. *Psychosocial process issues in child mental health* 3:7–13.

Registered Nurses Association of British Columbia, British Columbia Council of Licensed Practical Nurses, & Registered Psychiatric Nurse Association of British Columbia. n.d. *Nurse-client relationships: A discussion paper on preventing abuse of clients and expectations for professional behaviour*. Vancouver, BC.

Reite, M. 1990. Touch, attachment and health: Is there a relationship? *In Touch: The foundation of experience*, edited by K. E. Barnard and T. B. Brazelton. Madison, WI: International Universities Press, Inc.

Resch, Ruth C., Roy K. Lillesov, Helen M. Schur, and Thelma Mihalov. 1977. Infant day care as a treatment intervention. *Child Psychiatry and Human Development* 7 (3):147–155.

Rogoff, Barbara. 1990. *Apprenticeship in thinking: Cognitive development in social context*. New York and Oxford: Oxford University Press.

———. 2003. *The cultural nature of human development*. Oxford: Oxford University Press.

Roiphe, Anne. 1996. *Fruitful: Living the contradictions: A memoir of modern motherhood*. New York: Penguin.

Rowe, Deborah, Barbara Early, and Diane Loubier. 1994. Facilitating the distinctive role of infant and toddler teachers. In *New perspectives in early childhood teacher education: Bringing practitioners into the debate*, edited by S. Goffin and D. Day. New York: Teachers College Press.

Ruddick, Sarah. 1989. *Maternal thinking: Towards a politics of peace*. New York: Ballantine Books.

Ryan, S. M., C. Oschner, and C. Genishi. 2001. Miss Nelson is missing! Teacher sightings in research on teaching. In *Embracing identities in early childhood education: Diversity and possibilities*, edited by S. Grieshaber and C. Cannella. New York: Teachers College Press.

Scheper-Hughes, Nancy. 1992. *Death without weeping: The violence of everyday life in Brazil*. Berkeley, CA: University of California Press.

Schon, Donald A. 1987. *Educating the reflective practitioner*. San Francisco: Jossey-Bass.

———. ed. 1991. *The reflective turn: Case studies in and on educational practice*. New York: Teachers College Press.

Schradin, Carsten, Dee Ann Reeder, Sally Mendoa, and Gustl Anenberger. 2003. Prolactin and paternal care: Comparison of three species of monogamous new world monkeys. *Journal of Comparative Psychology* 117 (2):166–175.

Schultz, Thomas. 1994. Listening to teachers to improve the profession. In *New perspectives in early childhood teacher education: Bringing practitioners into the debate*, edited by S. Goffin and D. Day. New York: Teachers College Press.

Shamas, S. 1997. *A trilogy of performance*. Toronto: The Mercury Press.

Shepherd, Ray, Jennifer Jones, and Helen Taylor Robinson, eds. 1996. *Thinking about children, D. W. Winnicott*. Reading, MA: Addison-Wesley.

Shonkoff, Jack, and Deborah Phillips, eds. 2000. *From neurons to neighborhoods: The science of early childhood development*. Washington, DC: National Academy Press.

Silin, Jonathan G. 1997. The pervert in the classroom. In *Making a place for pleasure in early childhood education*, edited by J. Tobin. New Haven: Yale University Press.

Smith, Dorothy E. 1987. *The everyday world as problematic: A feminist sociology*. Toronto: University of Toronto Press.

Steinhauer, Paul. 1999. How a child's early experiences affect development. *Interaction* 13 (1):15–22.

Sullivan, Susan, Kathy Bose, and Lise Levesque, eds. 1999. *Research connections Canada: Supporting children and families*. Ottawa: Canadian Child Care Federation.

Suransky, Valerie Polakow. 1983. *The erosion of childhood*. Chicago: University of Chicago Press.

Taylor, S. E., L. C. Klein, B. P. Lewis, T. L. Gruenwald, R. A. R. Gurung, and J. A. Updegraff. 2000. Female responses to stress: Tend and befriend, not fight or flight. *Psychological Review* 107 (3):410–429.

Thomas, A., and S. Chess. 1977. *Temperament and development*. New York: Brunner/Mazel.

Thompson, Audrey. 1998. Not the color purple: Black feminist lessons for educational caring. *Harvard Educational Review* 68 (4):522–554.

Tobin, Joseph, ed. 1997. *Making a place for pleasure in early childhood education*. New Haven: Yale University Press.

Tobin, Joseph, and Dana Davidson. 1990. The ethics of polyvocal ethnography: Empowering vs. textualizing children and teachers. *Qualitative studies in education* 3 (3):271–283.

Tobin, Joseph, David Wu, and Dana Davidson. 1989. *Preschool in three cultures: Japan, China, and the United States*. New Haven: Yale University Press.

Ulrich, Laurel Thatcher. 1990. *A midwife's tale: The life of Martha Ballard based on her diary 1785–1812*. New York: Vintage Books.

Vanier, Jean. 1998. *Becoming human*. Toronto: Anansi.

Waerness, Kari. 1996. The rationality of caring. In *Caregiving: Readings in knowledge, practice, ethics, and politics*, edited by S. Gordon, P. Benner, and N. Noddings. Philadelphia: University of Pennsylvania Press.

Walker, Margaret Urban. 1992. Moral understandings: Alternative epistemology for a feminist ethics. In *Explorations in feminist ethics: Theory and practice*, edited by E. B. Cole and S. Coultrap-McQuin. Bloomington, IN: Indiana University Press.

Walsh, D. J., J. J. Tobin, and M. E. Graue. 1993. The interpretive voice: Qualitative research in early childhood education. In *Handbook of research on the education of young children*, edited by B. Spodek. New York: Macmillan.

Werner, Emmy E. 1987. *Vulnerability and resiliency: A longitudinal study of Asian Americans from birth to age 30*. Paper read at International Society for the Study of Behavioural Development, Tokyo, Japan.

Werner, Emmy E., and Ruth S. Smith. 1982. *Vulnerable but invincible: A longitudinal study of resilient children and youth*. New York: McGraw-Hill.

Whitebrook, M., C. Howes, and D. A. Phillips. 1990. *Who cares? Child care teachers and the quality of care in America. The National Child Care Staffing Study*. Oakland, CA: Child Care Employee Project.

Whiting, B. B., and C. P. Edwards. 1988. *Children of different worlds: The formation of social behavior*. Cambridge, MA and London, England: Harvard University Press.

Wien, Carol Anne. 1995. *Developmentally appropriate practice in "real life": Stories of teacher practical knowledge*. New York: Teachers College Press.

———. 1996. Time, work, and developmentally appropriate practice. *Early Childhood Research Quarterly* 11:377–403.

Williams, Leslie R., and Doris Pronin Fromberg, eds. 1992. *Encyclopedia of early childhood education*. New York and London: Garland.

Winnicott, D. W. 1987. *The child, the family, and the outside world*. Reading, MA: Addison-Wesley.

Wright, S. 2001. Closing our eyes very tightly: Attachment theory in the lives of children and other people. *The First Years: New Zealand Journal of Infant and Toddler Education* 3 (2):14–18.

Yelland, Nicola J., ed. 2000. *Promoting meaningful learning: Innovations in educating early childhood professionals*. Washington, DC: National Association for Young Children.

Yonemura, Margaret V. 1994. Accomplishing my work as a teacher educator: Hopes, practices, supports, and constraints. In *New perspectives in early childhood teacher education: Bringing practitioners into the debate*, edited by S. Goffin and D. Day. New York: Teachers College Press.

Young-Bruehl, Elisabeth, and Faith Bethelard. 2000. *Cherishment: A psychology of the heart*. New York: The Free Press.

Zeanah, C. H., O. K. Mammen, and A. F. Lieberman. 1993. Disorders of attachment. In *Handbook of infant mental health*, edited by C. H. Zeanah. New York: The Guilford Press.

Zimmerman, Libby, and Laurie McDonald. 1995. Emotional availability in infants' relationships with multiple caregivers. *American Journal of Orthopsychiatry* 65 (1):147–152.

Index

Ainsworth, Mary
    Baltimore study, 19
    quality of attachment, 19
    relationship and healthy infant
        development, 81
    strange situation, 22
    stranger anxiety, 22
    work in Uganda, 18–19
alloparent
    definition, 2
    role of community members, 20, 32
Ames, Eleanor
    Romanian orphans, 26
attachment, 7–8
    abused children and, 19
    and trust, x
    Bowlby and, 15
    brain research and, 24–26
    connection to others through, 23
    criticism of, 19–20
    detachment, 10
    cultural influences on, 21–24
    impact of, on adults, 15–17, 157
    in family daycare, 57
    meaning to caregivers, 7
    mother-infant bond and, 18
    primary caregiving and, 37
    psychological, 15
    quality of, 19–23
    relationships, 18, 35
    secure, 23
    theory of, 17–21

to babies, 7, 9
to environments, 38, 138
unhealthy, 7, 10

babies and infants
    appropriate care of, 14
    as individuals, 31, 43
    attachment to environment, 138
    "babysitting", 132
    brain development of, 15
    complexity of infants, 86
    death of, 22
    desire to communicate, 86–87
    development of trust, 94
    different baby's cries, 85–86
    elicit emotions in caregivers, 4,
        82–84, 122, 157
    inadequate support for, 131
    influence of culture on, 9, 14, 21
    need to be touched, 107
    needs of, 2, 6, 21, 37, 45, 86, 98,
        109, 128, 147
    relationship and infant develop-
        ment, 81
    relationships with caregivers, 73, 82,
        151–153
    sensing tensions, 108
    strategies for survival of, 18, 21,
        26–27, 81, 157
    stress and attachment to, 25
Bali
    high contact culture, and attach-
        ment, 22–23

191